Walks & Rambles in

RHODE ISLAND

A park naturalist looks over relics of one of Beavertail Point's many shipwrecks.

Walks & Rambles in

RHODE ISLAND

A Guide to the Natural & Historic Wonders of the Ocean State

KEN WEBER

Backcountry Publications
Woodstock, Vermont

An Invitation to the Reader

If you find that conditions have changed along these walks, please let the author and publisher know so that corrections may be made in future printings. Address all correspondence to:

Editor
Walks and Rambles Series
Backcountry Publications
P.O. Box 175
Woodstock, VT 05091

Library of Congress Cataloging-in-Publication Data
Weber, Ken
  Walks and rambles in Rhode Island.

  1. Walking — Rhode Island — Guide-books. 2. Rhode Island — Description and travel — 1981 — — Guide-books. I. Title
GV199.42.R4W44   1986   917.45'0443   85-26843
ISBN 0-942440-28-5 (pbk.)

© 1986 by Ken Weber
Fourth printing, updated 1990
Published by Backcountry Publications
A division of The Countryman Press, Inc.
Woodstock, Vermont 05091
Printed in the United States of America

Design by Ann Aspell
Maps and calligraphy by Alex Wallach
Photographs by the author

For Bettie, my favorite companion on the trails. Through her, I learned how much more interesting, more memorable, each walk becomes when shared with somebody special.

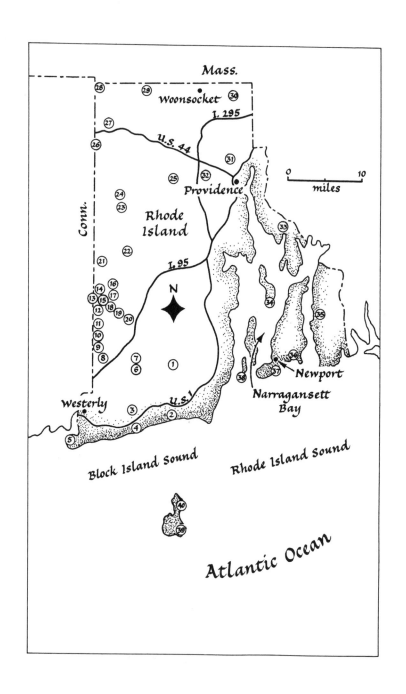

Mass.

Woonsocket

I. 295

U.S. 44

Providence

Conn.

Rhode
Island

I. 95

N

Westerly

U.S. 1

Newport

Narragansett
Bay

Block Island Sound

Rhode Island Sound

Atlantic Ocean

0   10
miles

Contents

Introduction

It's been more than 15 years since I first "discovered" the walking places of Rhode Island. That discovery led to a where-to hiking guide called *25 Walks in Rhode Island*, which consisted of detailed descriptions of some of my favorite trails. That book's acceptance told me there are many others who appreciate these trails just as much.

Since then, instead of becoming weary of rewalking familiar trails, I've become more fascinated. Trails change; there are always new features to find and examine. And there are always more places to explore.

Changes in trails — both good and bad changes — and the discovery of exciting new places to walk are two prime reasons for this new book. In preparing this book, I rewalked all 25 of the trails in the original book, then added 15 new routes. This book, then, provides a total of 40 trails, enough to keep the casual walker busy for a good many months.

As always, a strong effort was made to include a wide variety of walks in length and difficulty as well as geographic location, terrain, and interesting features. In short, these trails offer something for everyone.

There are island walks and bird walks, strolls on beaches and strenuous climbs through rocky ravines, looks at hidden mill ruins and a glimpse of 19th-century mansions. Some walks are short and easy; others require several hours and a good bit of stamina. Something for everyone.

The walks are arranged geographically, starting with one of the state's most special places, the Great Swamp, then going clockwise around the southwestern, western, northern and eastern areas before finally concluding with another unique spot, Block Island.

In between are the beaches of Ninigret and Napatree, the vast forests along the western border, the quiet woods and fields in the northwestern corner, the rocky bluffs of Diamond Hill, the close-to-the-city parks of Lincoln Woods and Dame Farm, the wildlife sanctuaries and islands of Narragansett Bay, and the famed Cliff Walk in Newport.

Most of the walks are loops, enabling you to return to the point where you began. Some, however, are one-way walks, making it necessary to leave another car at your terminus unless planning to retrace your steps. It is important that you read the descriptions before starting out in order to best prepare yourself; whether to bring lunch, what to wear, how much time to allow, etc.

With each trail description, distances and approximate walking times are provided, along with notes on the difficulty and, usually, the best time of year for choosing specific trails. Often it is possible to link trails and do more than one in an outing, and where trails connect that information is included.

The walking times are based on my own pace, which is fairly brisk but with numerous stops at places of interest. Many experienced hikers could do these walks in far less time, but I don't consider walking a competitive sport, nor an endurance event. Those who plunge through the woods, never stopping, looking neither left nor right, miss far too much. There is so much beauty, history and wildlife along these routes it would be a shame not to see as much of it as possible.

Sketch maps of each walk are included to help you visualize the route I describe. The following standard map symbols are used:

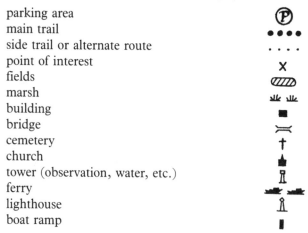

parking area	ⓟ
main trail	••••
side trail or alternate route	• • • •
point of interest	✕
fields	⬚
marsh	⅍ ⅍
building	▪
bridge	⪩
cemetery	†
church	⛪
tower (observation, water, etc.)	⎕
ferry	⛴
lighthouse	⛯
boat ramp	▮

Those wishing more detailed maps should obtain U.S. Geological Survey topographic sheets (available at many sporting goods stores). In addition, the Rhode Island Department of Environmental Management prints maps of its management areas and the Audubon Society of Rhode Island can provide maps of some of its properties.

2

I hope you will find that this is a book of far more than 40 walks. To really know these trails, you should walk them in each season. A woods path is completely different in snow than in summer. Why choose between wildflowers in spring and glorious autumn foliage? Enjoy both. Also, if you walk the routes in reverse direction you will get still another perspective. So instead of 40 walks, you can make hundreds from these trails.

Putting together this book required walking hundreds of miles in a relatively short time, but it was a labor of love. I found Rhode Island's footpaths no less intriguing now than when first seen many years ago. If anything, knowing them better only makes them more enjoyable, like revisiting a cherished place where the memories are all good. I hope you will feel the same.

1. Great Swamp

*A walk around a wildlife marsh
to see holly trees and ospreys*

Hiking distance: 5½ miles
Hiking time: 3-3½ hours

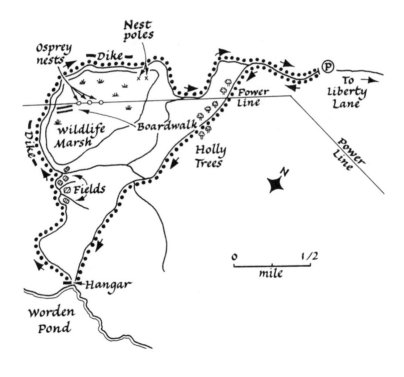

ONE OF THE PRIMARY REASONS FOR CHOOSING
one walk over another is the chance to see something different. At
the Great Swamp in South Kingstown, you'll see several things not
normally found elsewhere, particularly the holly trees and the ospreys.

There are not many places more interesting for those who see
hiking as more than mere walking. The route described here is an
easy 5½-mile loop that runs through a dense woodland, visits a
large pond, then wanders by management fields and follows a dike
around an intriguing wildlife marsh. For those who so desire, there
also is a boardwalk directly across the marsh, nearly under the
power-line poles upon which the ospreys nest. The entire route
could be walked in a couple of hours but usually takes much longer
— there are so many reasons for lingering.

The 3,000-acre Great Swamp is one of the state management
areas that caters to sportsmen, but in doing so also contributes
immensely to the proliferation of all kinds of wildlife. Once this
place was the last stronghold of Rhode Island's native Indians, now
it is home to many plants and animals that have been virtually
obliterated elsewhere in the state.

The best time to make this walk is early spring, even though the
swamp roads are open to walkers all year. In autumn and early
winter, the area teems with hunters. In summer, poison ivy, mosquitoes, black flies, and the heat associated with most swamps can
add up to discomfort. But in early spring, the place is a delight.
Be sure to bring binoculars and perhaps a camera with a telephoto
lens.

ACCESS

To reach the Great Swamp, take RI 138 to the village of West
Kingston, turn west onto Liberty Lane and follow the road until it
ends at a railroad track. Then go left on a gravel lane about a mile,
passing the office and maintenance buildings, and park in a small
lot at a barred gateway.

TRAIL

You will walk on access roads throughout this hike. The woods
are both damp and dense, in most cases nearly impenetrable. But

there is no need to leave the roads; you can see so much from flat, open lanes.

At the start, tall trees shade the road and the understory of young dogwoods, blackberries, huckleberries, pepperbush, and blueberries adds colorful variety. In spring, you are likely to see violets beside the road. In summer, there will be the pretty purple flowers called deer grass, and in winter, the bright red berries of the black alder practically glow against the stark background.

On spring walks, you can expect to see and hear catbirds, towhees, orioles, and other songbirds all along this route, at least until you reach the wildlife marsh, where waterfowl, ospreys, and swallows take over.

In less than half a mile, the road splits. If you want only to see the marsh, you can take the right fork. For this walk, however, keep to the left. You will be returning on the other path.

The feature of the next section is the holly. These trees, so eagerly sought at Christmastime, are abundant along this road — you can find more here than anywhere else in the state. Look but don't touch; they are protected by state law. They are especially vibrant in winter when red berries embellish the shiny green foliage, but they also stand out in early spring, before the surrounding trees and bushes open their leaves.

After crossing a clearing cut for the power line, you return to a drier forest rich with ferns. Without leaving the road, you can find ferns of half a dozen varieties. Mixed in are creeping jenny and prince's pine, two club mosses also protected by law. And guarding the plants are thorny brambles of greenbrier.

You will pass two cutoff trails, first one to the right and then a narrow path to the left. Stay on the main gravel lane. When you enter an area dotted with huge boulders and ledges, you are nearing Worden Pond, a shallow, 1,000-acre pond that forms the southern boundary of the management area. The road ends beside a federally-owned seaplane hangar at the water's edge, but you can take a few minutes and look over the pond, a popular fishing spot.

To the right, as you approach the hangar, you will see a more obscure trail going over a boggy area. When you are ready to leave the pond, take this lane. Only the first few yards are wet, and in a short distance the overgrown road opens into a grassy, pleasant path that winds uphill through the woods. It leads to numerous small fields planted in grain or left in meadows for the benefit of wildlife.

7

At each field, there is a birdhouse put up for bluebirds, but in most cases the residents are tree swallows.

The walking can get a bit tricky here. A general rule is to go left at each fork. You will soon emerge on a gravel road. Turn left again, heading downhill, and in minutes you will find yourself on the dike built in the 1950s to create the 140-acre marsh.

This may be the best segment of the walk, especially for those who like birds. Numerous wood duck houses dot the marsh, and swimming among the lilies and other aquatic plants are usually ducks, swans and geese. Herons and kingfishers are common, and swallows fill the air (and most of the duck houses).

What is likely to capture your attention, however, are the ospreys, the big, fish-eating hawks once close to extinction in New England. To the right, you can see the string of powerline poles across the marsh, and balanced atop many of the poles are the ospreys' bulky nests. No other place in the state has an osprey population that rivals the Great Swamp's, and the grassy dike offers a superb place to sit and watch the graceful birds.

In early spring, while the ospreys are adding sticks to their nests, you can approach close enough for good photographs on the boardwalk that runs under the lines — if you don't mind wires in your pictures — but you may be prohibited from using the boardwalk during the brooding season in order to prevent disturbing the parent birds.

Along the left side of the curving dike is shallow water that features turtles, frogs, and wildflowers. Beyond the stream is a junglelike tangle of dense undergrowth.

Shortly before the end of the dike, you can see two more poles with platforms on top in the marsh on your right. These were put up expressly for the ospreys and on my last visit one was in use. With a telephoto lens, you can photograph the action at this nest, and will have no problems with wires. It's a perfect place to linger before heading back into the woods.

The final segment swings slightly uphill, passes under the power lines briefly, and rejoins the road you began on. A left turn and short walk takes you back to your car.

2. Trustom Pond

One of the best birding walks through a former farm to a coastal sanctuary

Hiking distance: 3 miles
Hiking time: 1½-2 hours

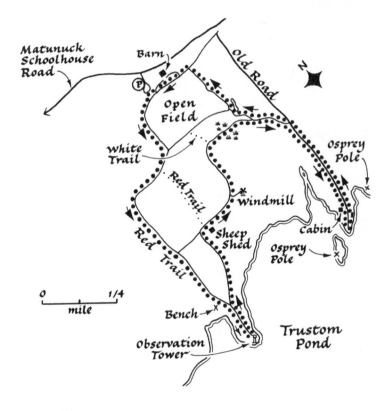

Matunuck Schoolhouse Road

Barn

Old Road

N

P

Open Field

White Trail

Red Trail

Osprey Pole

Windmill

Cabin

Red Trail

Sheep Shed

Osprey Pole

0 — 1/4 mile

Bench

Observation Tower

Trustom Pond

TRUSTOM POND IS FOR THE BIRDS — AND THAT'S
the way the people who manage the place want it. On this walk,
you will see a great variety of birds and will note just how much
effort has been put into making this coastal sanctuary appealing to
them.

Trustom Pond National Wildlife Refuge encompasses far more
than the saltwater pond of its name. The refuge includes open fields
and abandoned pastures, thickets of surging bushes and low-lying
marshes. You can visit each terrain in this 3-mile walk, and as a
bonus, look over a tiny cabin, a sheep shed, and a windmill left
over from the days when this was a thriving farm belonging to the
Alfred Morse family. The family eventually donated the farm and
property to the U.S. Fish and Wildlife Service.

Throughout the area, there are birdhouses and nesting aids for
birds ranging from purple martins to ospreys, from bluebirds to
wood ducks. There also are many descriptive signs that indicate
how certain plants and habitats benefit specific birds. On a good
day, perhaps a sunny morning in May, you can easily find 40 or 50
species of birds on this easy, comfortable ramble.

ACCESS

To reach the refuge, take U.S. 1 in South Kingstown to Moonstone
Beach Road. Follow that road 1 mile and turn right on Matunuck
Schoolhouse Road. The refuge entrance is 0.7 mile on the left.

TRAIL

From the parking area, a fenced walkway leads first to a kiosk,
which describes the sanctuary and where you can obtain a trail
map, then goes through an area of thick, young bushes to an open
field.

Your birding begins immediately. In this first set of bushes you
are likely to find warblers, catbirds, thrashers and other songbirds.
As soon as you reach the open field, there will be bobolinks, meadowlarks and perhaps a hunting marsh hawk.

The refuge paths are called the Marsh Trail, blazed in red, and
the Swan Point Trail, marked in white. They run together across
the hay field, then split at a stone wall. Go right, on the red trail
first; you will pick up the white trail later.

10

The red trail quickly divides; continue walking west, on the right fork. Soon, the path swings left and goes through an area filled with bushes and small trees. There are a great many wild fruits growing here — blueberries, raspberries, wild cherries, viburnums — and consequently birds are abundant. Robins, catbirds, thrashers, orioles, and many, many others congregate here in summer.

Stay on the path (passing a cutoff to the left) as it runs through this bird haven. At a second cutoff, you will see a wooden bench. You will eventually take this path, but first follow the main lane out onto a point that reaches into Trustom Pond. There are several spots from which you can view the water. Usually, there are terns, geese, ducks, and swans on the pond, and if you look to the left you can see a small island on which a pole and platform have been installed for ospreys. The platform is currently in use and you may want to linger here, watching the graceful fishhawks.

At the very tip of the point, there is a wooden observation tower from which you can look across the pond to Moonstone, the barrier beach on the far side, which is also a bird refuge.

Trustom Pond offers a quiet refuge for waterfowl, songbirds, and contemplative strollers.

When ready to resume walking, go back up the trail to the fork at the bench. The cutoff, now on your right, is narrow and winding. It runs through another thicket of young trees, including several apples, and follows a stone wall briefly before emerging on a grassy lane. This is the cutoff you passed earlier. Go a few steps to the right and you will reach the sheep shed, now used for storage. The pastures both in front of the shed and behind it are steadily being taken over by bushes and wildflowers.

From the shed, the red trail runs directly north, toward the refuge headquarters, but to see the windmill and then hook up with the white trail, follow a mowed lane to the left (as you face the shed). This lane runs along a wall that divides the pastures, then swings left at a marshy woodlot. At this curve, go right on a narrow path a few yards to the windmill, still spinning in the breeze although no longer pumping water for the now vanished sheep.

From the windmill, the lane runs along the woods edge, then curls slightly to the right, where it meets the white trail (although there are no signs here) coming in from the large hayfield. At this junction, take a right turn on a narrow path that runs through the damp woods, crossing the wettest area on a wooden walkway.

In a few yards, you will pass a trail angling in from the left. You will walk this trail later, but for now, continue straight ahead to an old road that follows a line of trees and still another stone wall. Turn right on this shady, picturesque road and follow it out to a second point in Trustom Pond.

This point is particularly idyllic, with a tiny cabin, built by the Morses, surrounded by apple trees, sea breezes, and more songbirds. There are several interpretive signs here and a bench that offers good viewing across the water at a second platform pole put up for ospreys. From the tip of the point, where you'll see trees with unique, twisted forms from the constant buffeting of the wind, you can expect to find more geese, ducks, and shorebirds.

When you return north on the road, take the path toward the marsh and then follow the cutoff, now on your right. It curls around the left edge of a pretty little pond equipped with a pier, wood duck houses, and a martin house. Whether you see wood ducks or not, you are fairly sure to see turtles and frogs.

Beyond the pond, follow the lane across the hayfield to a roadway just behind the barn area. Go left on this road until reaching the fenced walkway where you began. Chances are, the warblers and catbirds will still be there, waiting for you.

3. Burlingame Park

The greatest variety of plant life, including the elusive holly tree.

Hiking distance: 7¾ miles
Hiking time: 3½-4 hours

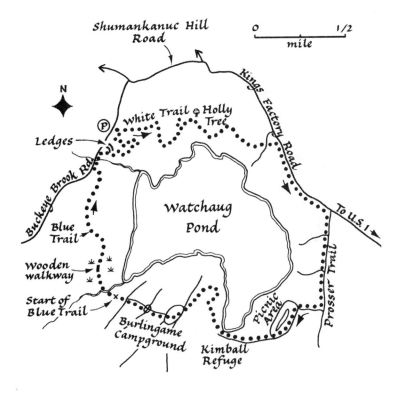

Shumankanuc Hill Road

0 ———— 1/2
mile

N

White Trail ⚬ Holly Tree

Ⓟ

Ledges

Buckeye Brook Rd.

Kings Factory Road

Watchaug Pond

To U.S. 1

Blue Trail

Prosser Trail

wooden walkway

Start of Blue Trail

×

Burlingame Campground

Kimball Refuge

Picnic Area

VARIETY IS THE THEME FOR THIS WALK. THERE is something for everyone on this long loop around Watchaug Pond in Burlingame State Park in Charlestown. You will walk through dense forests and on paved roadways. You will visit a busy campground and a quiet bird sanctuary. You will take an elevated walkway over a swamp and circle rugged rock ledges.

Along the way, you also will see a greater variety of plant life than on most other walks, ranging from tiny mosses and lichens up through ferns and wintergreen, through thickets of mountain laurel, rhododendron and blueberries to towering pines, hemlocks, beeches and oaks. Also, at one point, the sharp-eyed can see a rare holly tree.

The entire walk is within the state park, except for a section on the east side of Watchaug Pond, where you must leave the woods because of private property. The walk is about 7¾ miles and will take 3½ to 4 hours, plus time for a lunch break.

ACCESS

To reach the start on Buckeye Brook Road from northern Rhode Island, take RI 91 to the little community of Wood River Junction. Drive south on Kings Factory Road to Shumankanuc Road, go right 0.3 mile to Buckeye Brook Road, then left just under a mile to a woods road going off to the right. You can park here; the trail starts on the opposite side of the paved road. If coming from U.S. 1 on the south, take Kings Factory Road 3 miles north and turn left on Shumankanuc.

TRAIL

Follow the white-blazed trail into the woods. In a few minutes, you'll see a blue-marked trail on your right; this is your return path. Stay on the white trail, which soon crosses a dirt road and runs through a grove of dead and dying pines. Watch carefully; the main path continues, but in minutes the white-blazed trail makes an abrupt right turn into dense forest.

For some distance you weave around low ledges, alternately following overgrown lanes and cutting through the woods. It is shortly after you pass through a hemlock grove, turn left off one of the lanes, then take a quick right that you may find the holly tree. It's

14

about 20 feet off the trail, on the left. Perhaps 25 feet tall, it is a beautiful specimen of a plant rarely found anywhere in the state. But don't cut twigs or disturb it in any way; holly trees are protected by law. The walking in this area is not difficult; despite the ledges, boulders, and stone walls, you do virtually no rock-scrambling. In winter, at a point where the trail makes a sharp turn left, you can glimpse Watchaug Pond through the trees on the right. You won't see it again for a few miles.

When you emerge on a paved road, you have gone about 1.8 miles. The trail goes across, through a narrow woodlot and reaches another road. This is Kings Factory Road, and you will follow it to the right for 0.3 mile to Prosser Trail, also paved. Go right on this road, past a chain-link fence and two private roads, and follow the white blazes as they turn right on still another roadway back into the park. Straight ahead is a parking lot and a large picnic area beside the pond.

The trail swings left, along the edge of the parking lot, and follows a road along the southwestern shore of the pond until you enter Kimball Wildlife Sanctuary, owned by the Audubon Society of Rhode Island. In all, you walk slightly more than 1½ miles on pavement before following the white blazes into the bushes just inside the sanctuary. The trail barely skirts the edge of Kimball, one of the favorite places in Rhode Island for birders. The trail runs closer to Watchaug Pond here than at any other point, and you can take side paths to the water. You have walked nearly four miles and a pause beside the 934-acre pond can be inviting.

You will be in Kimball refuge only briefly before entering the sprawling Burlingame Camping Area, the state's largest campground. You must be careful here, particularly when the trail goes into a large, open field. The next blaze is across the field, on a rock beside a row of telephones at the camp store and coffee shop. From there, cross the circular driveway and pick up blazes along the middle campground road. You then walk through the heart of the camping area, a bustling little city of tents and campers in summer. Still, it's a pleasant walk with tall, straight pines on both sides. When the pavement ends (look for an outhouse on the left), the trail continues on a level, grassy lane into the forest.

This is a delightful segment. Do not be concerned when the blazes suddenly become blue rather than white. You will see a sign saying N/S Trail; this is to be part of a long-planned North–South Trail running the entire length of Rhode Island from Burrillville to the ocean. At present, it is not completed, but you will see N/S signs frequently from here to the end of this walk.

When the grassy lane turns left, go straight ahead and soon you will be on the wooden walkway that a Young Adult Conservation Corps built in 1981. It is about two feet wide and, for the most part, about three feet above a swampy area. For about 200 yards, you get a unique look at the plant and animal life of a swamp. It is one of the highlights of this trail.

For the next half-mile, you walk an open, grassy lane, then cut through the woods and emerge on a paved road. This is Buckeye Brook Road, and if you continued to the right you would reach your car in about another half-mile. As soon as the road crosses a stream, however, the trail swings back into the forest on the right, and wanders at the base of several high, picturesque ledges.

The final section of the walk is a series of turns and switchbacks, several accompanied by wooden arrows on trees. When you finally see the intersection with the white-blazed path you walked earlier, turn left and you will be at your car in moments.

4. Ninigret Beach

A barrier beach walk with wide variety of ocean birds and seashore plants

Hiking distance: 6½ miles
Hiking time: 2½-3 hours

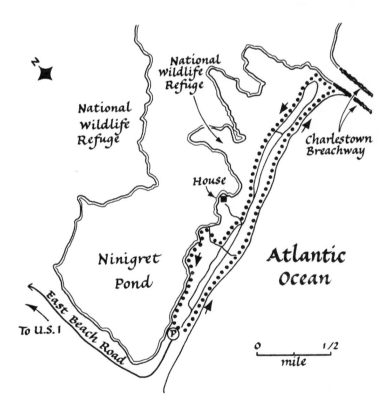

National
Wildlife
Refuge

National
Wildlife
Refuge

Charlestown
Breachway

House

Ninigret
Pond

Atlantic
Ocean

To U.S. 1

East Beach Road

0   1/2
mile

THE LONG MILES OF BEACH AND SAND IN THE

Ninigret Conservation Area offer extremes in weather and walking conditions. In summer, you have to guard against sunburn; in winter it is a place of icy wind blasts.

But there are many reasons for making this walk, among them the many seashore plants and the ocean birds you are likely to see. Your will walk the beach to a breachway, then return along the interior sand dunes and the shore of a shallow salt pond.

Ninigret, in Charlestown, is a state-owned barrier beach about 3 miles along. Since it is the first line of defense against storms that sweep in from Block Island Sound, it is extremely important to the southern Rhode Island coastline. It also protects Ninigret Pond, the cove known for its crabs, clams, and other aquatic life.

ACCESS

The only road to the conservation area (not to be confused with the more visable nearby Ninigret National Wildlife Refuge) is East Beach Pond. It is reached via U.S. 1, just east of RI 216. If you go in summer, be sure to arrive early. The small parking area fills quickly with swimmers and sunbathers. From Memorial Day to Labor Day, there is a fee for parking. In the off-season, entry is free.

TRAIL

From the parking lot, cross the ridge of sand to the beach and begin walking east — to your left. In swimming season, this first section is likely to be jammed, but proceed to the edge of the water (firm sand is much easier to walk on) and begin. In a matter of minutes, you will be beyond the crowds and after that you will meet only occasional walkers, joggers and surf fishermen. In the off-season, Jeeps, dune buggies, and other recreational vehicles sometimes roar by you but are not a major problem.

On a clear day, you can see Block Island, lying about 12 miles offshore. It seems much closer, but distances over water can be deceiving. For instance, as you look east down the beach, you can make out the dark line of Charlestown breach extending into the water. This is your goal. The line is a mass of large rocks and appears to be just a short stroll away. Those rocks are, in fact, 3 miles off.

Still, it is a most pleasant 3 miles. The beach is smooth and clean.

A ridge of dune grass strives to hold the shifting sands of Ninigret Beach in place.

The few pebbles at the tideline glisten brightly as each wave washes over them, leaving the small stones polished and pretty. The sea glimmers in the sunshine, and the waves roll in inexorably, breaking white on the sand. On calm days, you find yourself playing tag with the erratic breakers, like sandpipers, as you try to stay dry. On stormier days, you retreat up the beach and watch as the waves pound the sand in relentless fury.

Bring your binoculars, because many birds ride the waves a short distance offshore. Look for grebes, loons, mergansers, scoters, and scaup during the colder months. Petrels often skim the waves in winter as do terns in the summer. During spring and fall migrations, numerous canvasbacks, goldeneyes, and other ducks rest here, and the beach at times is alive with sandpipers, plovers, and other shorebirds. Gulls, of course, inhabit the beach in all seasons.

On your left, throughout the 3 miles, is the ridge that separates the beach from the pond. Like most barrier beaches, it is fragile and you will see areas where pines have been planted to prevent erosion. There also are many bushes and grasses atop the ridge, along with sections of storm fences, that help hold the dunes in place. Walkers are advised not to climb the ridge; even a few crushed plants can escalate erosion.

When you reach the end of the beach, climb the pile of roughcut stones. It is an ideal place to rest while watching the boats cruise through the channel. On the opposite side there often are fishermen, and you are likely to see campers parked at the western end of Charlestown Beach.

To begin the return walk, approximately 3½ miles long and at times more tedious because of soft sand, take the breachway rocks over the ridge. You are facing north and looking over Ninigret Pond at the abandoned naval air station that is now part of the developing wildlife refuge.

Two sand roads that run the length of the dune end here, amid the plants of a salt meadow. Seaside roses thrive in dense thickets, decorating the spot with pinkish purple and white blossoms in early summer and huge orange rosehips in fall. The low-lying, pale green bushes known as dusty millers are easy to find, too, as are bayberries and the vining beach peas. Nearer the water, tall reeds called pampas grass ripple in the breeze.

Egrets, herons, ibises and a wide variety of sandpipers frequent the pond edges, and you are likely to see swans or geese resting on the calm waters. However, the tangles of bushes and the swampy terrain make walking the pond shore difficult here. Instead, follow one of the sand roads. They run parallel to each other, and the only difference between them is that the one on the right offers slightly better views of the pond.

You pass through an area designated part of the wildlife refuge, where the roads are lined with wire barriers on both sides. A short time later, you pass a house perched on a knoll on your right, just above the pond.

If you tire of walking in the soft sand, you can take one of the cuts in the ridge and return to the beach. At a well-used cutoff road, however, you can swing to the right and follow the pond the final mile. The walking is easier and more interesting.

You are likely to flush many flocks of sandpipers and will see swallows and other birds swooping over the water. Bits of shells line the shore and you can expect to see people wading in the shallow pond (average depth is four feet) seeking the abundant quahaugs and littlenecks.

You may want to try clamming yourself before reaching the parking lot, and even if you are not interested in clams, the thought of letting that water cool off your feet after 6½ miles in the sand can be almost irresistible.

5. Napatree Point

Three miles of sand and sea — bird life, military history, and a glimpse of what a hurricane can do

Hiking distance: 3 miles
Hiking time: 2 hours

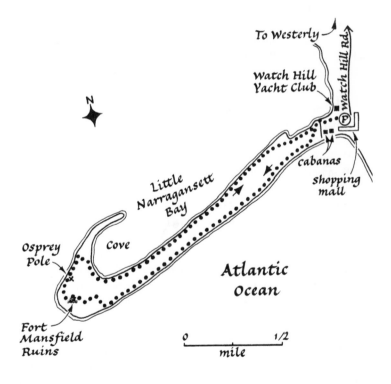

SAVE THIS WALK FOR AUTUMN OR WINTER,

when the swimmers and sunbathers have gone and the boating activity around the nearby Watch Hill Yacht Club has diminished. Then, Napatree Point is an interesting place indeed.

Napatree is as far west as you can go in Rhode Island and farther south than any other mainland point. It reaches out into Little Narragansett Bay below Westerly like a slim, J-shaped finger.

ACCESS

To reach Napatree Point, take RI 1A to the village of Avondale, then follow Watch Hill Road until it reaches a little shopping mall at the water's edge. You can see the yacht club on the right. Park in the mall and walk the road that runs by the yacht club, past private cabanas on your left, to a fence barrier. There you'll find two signs, one advising you that this is an osprey nesting area and the other, put up by the Napatree Point Conservation Association, that invites walkers but asks you to stay on the trails in order to preserve the delicate status of the dune grass and other vegetation.

TRAIL

All barrier beaches are fragile and Napatree is one of the most fragile. Once it extended much farther into the sea, but the hurricane of 1938 broke through it. The devastation was immense, with several lives lost and practically all the houses and cottages that then lined the beach being demolished. Now there are no buildings out on the point, and great care should be taken not to walk on or disturb the vegetation along the center. It literally holds Napatree in place against the forces of the sea.

In addition to its osprey nest, which is on a platform atop a pole at the far end of the point, there are areas roped off for the ground nests of terns, so extra care is necessary when visiting this area. Also, leave your dogs at home if you walk here in summer; they can quickly destroy a tern nesting colony.

The fence barrier leaves room at the right end for you to enter, and immediately you have a choice. A trail runs right along the water and another path goes left over the ridge, between snow fences, toward the sea. Take the left path, even though walking in the soft sand is tedious. In a few moments you'll be facing the ocean and walking near the water, where the sand is firmer and less tiring.

This is the area most crowded in summer, but the entire beach is usually deserted in winter, except for a few strollers and an occasional jogger. During September and October, you are likely to find a number of birders on the point, for Napatree is a key spot in the migratory flyway of hawks. When conditions are right, hundreds of hawks of half a dozen varieties will pass over the point in a single day.

For more than a mile, you can walk a curving shoreline, gulls and other seabirds riding the waves on your left, starfish and bits of shells on the beach at your feet, and the low ridge with its beach plums, dusty millers, and other bushes and grasses on your right.

When you finally reach a jumble of large rocks in the water near the point's end, follow a sand path uphill into a thicket of blackberries, bittersweet, and other bushes on the ridge and you'll find something most of the summertime visitors know nothing about — the remains of Fort Mansfield.

The fort was built around the turn of the century but almost immediately was found to be indefensible and soon was abandoned and eventually dismantled. All that remains now are a few graffiti-marred low walls and concrete steps, a room or two, and the round holes for the gun turrets, all hidden from shoreline view by the vines and bushes.

However, from the fort, you have a good view of the osprey nest on the harbor side of Napatree. It's also an excellent place to find songbirds that often dally here during migration, as well as a handy spot from which to view the hawk migration.

During nesting season, walkers are advised to stay away from the osprey nest — the big, fish-eating hawks once were seriously declining in numbers and nest platforms are helping their comeback — but in fall or winter you can take a path to the rocky shore beside the pole. Among the rocks, you may find sandpipers and shorebirds and there often are loons or cormorants just offshore.

A short distance beyond the osprey nest, you can take a narrow path over the low ridge to a smooth cove. If you continue walking the outside shoreline, you'll go onto the dead-end curl of the J and will have to come back to the cove, adding perhaps a half-mile or more to your walk.

The cove is interesting because its shallow, calm water offers refuge for ducks and mergansers and also for the many jellyfish you can see as you walk along. The footing on the harbor side of

Napatree isn't as smooth as on the sea side, more gravel than sand, but it's still an easy walk back, past the yacht club and its flotilla of boats.

This can be a very busy place in summer, with boats of all sizes and descriptions coming and going, and boating enthusiasts will want to linger here just as birders often are reluctant to leave the point. By autumn, the boating activity declines dramatically but there are always some crafts moored in the shallow harbor, and the tranquil scene draws many photographers and artists.

The entire walk can be done in a couple of hours, but if you like seascapes, migratory birds, boats, and invigorating salt air, it could, and should, take much longer.

6. Carolina South

A walk for solitude and a bit of history

Hiking distance: 3 miles
Hiking time: 1½-2 hours

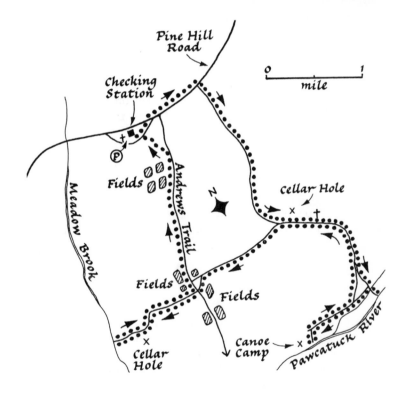

IF YOU LIKE SOLITUDE — A PLACE WHERE YOU can walk for miles among the trees and brooks and fields without meeting other people — then Carolina South might be ideal.

As long as you don't go in hunting season.

Carolina South is a walk through the southern section of the 1,500-acre Carolina Management Area in Richmond. It is only 3 miles long, but could easily be combined with Carolina North (see Walk 7) if you want more exercise. Or you could wander down a few more of the access roads.

The route described here, though short, is likely to keep you interested. You start near a tiny cemetery, pass another graveyard (surrounded by a picket fence) hidden far back in the woods, visit a couple of old cellar holes, take a look at a campsite for canoeists on the Pawcatuck River, pause in a clearing where apple and pear trees continue to survive long after abandonment, and walk along fields planted for the benefit of wildlife.

As with other management areas, this place teems with hunters in fall, when deer, grouse, and rabbits are sought, but for most of the rest of the year, Carolina South is left for the walker and an occasional horseman.

ACCESS

To reach the starting point from the northern part of the state, take RI 138 east (Exit 3 off I-95) to RI 112 just east of Hope Valley. Go south on RI 112 2.5 miles to Pine Hill Road, turn west (right) and proceed for 1.5 miles. On the left is a red hunter checking station with ample parking at its rear. If coming from the coastal area, go left on Pine Hill Road just north of the village of Carolina.

TRAIL

After parking behind the red building, walk around to the front and look over the tiny cemetery there. Dates on the stones indicate the last burial was more than 100 years ago. Shading the graves are several apple and pear trees, which add colorful blossoms in spring. It's a pretty, peaceful spot and sets the mood for this walk.

Walk east (back toward RI 112) on Pine Hill Road about 0.3 miles to find the access road on the right where you will enter the forest. A gravel lane at first, the road runs beneath tall pines and before long the surface is only pine needles and then grass. This road runs along the eastern boundary of the state property and you will see numerous Keep Out and No Trespassing signs on your left. As long as you stay on the road, you are okay.

When the lane makes a sweeping curve to the left, following a stone wall, you enter a clearing now being devoured by the surging woods. Wild grapes and greenbrier vines swarm over the rocks and logs, and saplings of a dozen species compete for growing space. Still holding their own are a few apple and pear trees, which bloom defiantly each spring and produce some small, misshapen fruit late each summer. They show this was a home site once, and off to the left of the trail you can find a cellar hole, now little more than a pile of tumbled stones.

Breaking off to the right at the clearing is another grassy lane. Later, this will be your route to the fields area. For now, stay on the main road. Soon you will see the cemetery surrounded with a faded, white picket fence. This graveyard is not as old as the one along Pine Hill Road; some stones are dated after 1900. The fence makes it unusual; most similar cemeteries are guarded by stone walls.

A few yards beyond the cemetery, the road forks. Take the left branch downhill, and then go left again at the next junction. Here you can cross a brook on a stone bridge and follow a narrow path to the Pawcatuck River. The path also turns left and runs out to an open field, but at that point it leaves state property. So after looking over the river, recross the bridge and take a left on a path that runs parallel to the brook, which soon empties into the river.

You quickly pass a lane coming in from the right (your return route) and you will follow a stone wall briefly. Beyond the wall you can see boulders and bedrock ledges back in the woods, one of the few rocky areas on this walk.

A cutoff trail to the left takes you to the canoe campsite and an outhouse. The camp is little more than a small clearing for tents and a rock-ringed fireplace, but offers a good view of the Pawcatuck and a place to linger.

The woods road past the camp eventually deadends at a fence, so retrace your steps east to the lane you passed earlier. Take it north (left), and go uphill until it rejoins your original road just below the cemetery.

After crossing the clearing, go left on the other lane you passed earlier. It is marked by a barrier of large stones placed there to prevent use by vehicles. Walking is permitted, however, and you can follow this lane through a mixed forest to the center of the management grounds.

When it emerges at a small field, look for a left fork that runs through another small woodlot to a larger field. Walk the edge of the field, to the left, to a gravel road. This is called Andrews Trail on management maps, and it cuts through the heart of the fields area. You can go left here and look over numerous grain and meadow parcels, or turn right and walk back to the checking station.

A third option is to cross the gravel road, walk the edge of a field, and look for a narrow lane that angles to the left into the woods. Just a few yards down this lane, hidden in a tangle of old lilacs and other bushes on the left, is a cellar hole that features a huge foundation of a center chimney.

The trail continues to a rocky crossing over a stream called Meadow Brook, and the stream is worth a look, but for return to your start, a backtracking to the gravel Andrews Trail is recommended.

After turning north on Andrews Trail, you are on the final segment. The road runs between open fields at first, then goes through a forest of mostly pines for some distance before reaching fields again. Off to the left is the checking station and your car.

7. Carolina North

Laurel, hemlocks, songbirds, and grouse, and perhaps a look at wild turkeys

Hiking distance: 4 miles
Hiking time: 2 hours

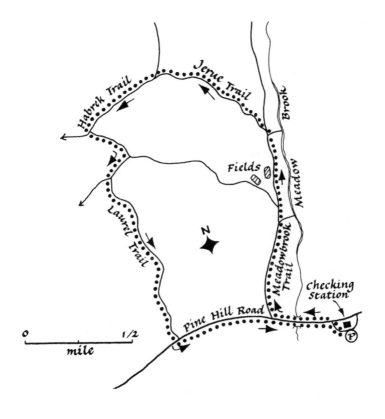

Habren Trail

Jerue Trail

Brook

Fields

Meadow

Laurel Trail

N

Meadowbrook Trail

Checking Station

Pine Hill Road

0   1/2
mile

P

SAVE THIS WALK FOR SOME BRIGHT MORNING in May. That's when a stroll through the northern segment of the Carolina Management Area in Richmond is most rewarding, because you will be fairly certain to hear and possibly see wild turkeys.

Absent from Rhode Island for more than 150 years, wild turkeys have been reestablished through a state stocking program, and nowhere are they more common than in the big forests of Carolina. Walking here offers other delights, too, but the turkeys make this place unique, especially in spring, when the gobblers are noisy.

This 4-mile walk is called Carolina North because it lies on the north side of Pine Hill Road, which slices through the 1,500-acre management area. There is another ramble called Carolina South (see Walk 6) on the opposite side of Pine Hill Road.

Carolina North's entire walk is on management access roads, some marked, some unmarked. You will start on perhaps the most commonly used road, then cut through the heart of the forest, and return on a virtually unused lane that returns you to Pine Hill Road. The loop can easily be done in 2 hours.

ACCESS

To reach the starting point for both Carolina walks from the northern part of the state, take RI 138 east (Exit 3 off I-95) to RI 112 just east of Hope Valley. Go south on RI 112 2.5 miles to Pine Hill Road, turn west (right) and proceed for 1.5 miles. On the left is a red hunter checking station with ample parking at its rear. If coming from the coastal area, go left on Pine Hill Road just north of the hamlet of Carolina.

TRAIL

From the checking station, walk Pine Hill Road a few yards west, cross a stream called Meadow Brook, and take the first gravel lane off to the right into the forest. Meadow Brook is a popular trout stream in spring and this lane, identified by a sign on a tree as Meadowbrook Trail, has several cutoffs to the stream for fishermen. The access roads are busy in fall as well, when hunters scatter through the woods in search of deer, grouse, and rabbits, and snowmobilers use them in winter.

Meadowbrook Trail is shaded by tall pines for the first half-mile, and in May, you are likely to hear numerous songbirds in the dense woods as well as the turkeys. There may also be grouse "drumming," calling potential mates with loud sounds created by beating the air with their wings.

Beyond the first fishermen's cutoff, you will pass a gravel lane that goes to the left. In this area, there are several small clearings — fields designed to attract and feed wildlife. When you reach the second cutoff to the stream (again on your right), there is a barway and a fork in the roadway. Go left (a sign calls this lane Jerue Trail) for a look at a section of forest undergoing management procedures.

This lane has less traffic than Meadowbrook, winds around much more, and is a bit more hilly. The forest, now being thinned considerably, is mostly second-growth hardwoods with a great deal of mountain laurel in the understory. Dogwoods will be blooming in May and there are numerous wildflowers and ferns along the trail.

You will pass networks of stone walls that indicate this was once farmland, then a huge old beech tree covered with carvings, most of them initials from the 1940s.

When you reach a barway at a lane junction, turn left. Now you are on Habrek Trail, although there are no signs here. Forest is thick on both sides, with many young pines crowding the trail. You will be walking mostly downhill. If it is May, you'll notice several old apple trees blossoming, an even more vibrant legacy to the vanished farmers than the many stone walls.

At the next junction, go left. Again, there are no signs. There are more old apple trees along this section, and many lovely pines. Now, you are walking slightly uphill. If you stayed on this lane, you would eventually return to Meadowbrook Trail, but it is better to turn right at the first opportunity so that you are not walking any trail twice.

The turn to the right has you going downhill, with a stone wall along the right side. In just a few minutes, you reach one more fork in an area where the forest has been thinned. Go left, heading slightly uphill. This is called Laurel Trail on management maps, and you will remain on it for more than a mile, all the way back to Pine Hill Road.

When you reach a grove of tall pines, the trail narrows considerably and the surface changes from gravel to pine needles and grass. For the rest of the way, this is a pleasant woods path all but abandoned by vehicles. In places, young pines are growing in the trail.

In other places, the lane cuts through stone walls in open woods. There are areas of large boulders and areas of exquisite hemlocks. And throughout the final mile, there are the laurel bushes that may make you want to return in June, when they will be in bloom.

You will emerge on the paved Pine Hill Road almost directly across from a home. Turn left, round a bend, and you will quickly reach the Meadowbrook Trail where you began. Your car is just ahead on the right.

8. Long Pond-Ell Pond

A strenuous walk to three ponds, a "cathedral" in the woods, and a "magnificent mile" of wild rhododendrons and hemlocks

Hiking distance: 4½ miles
Hiking time: 3 hours

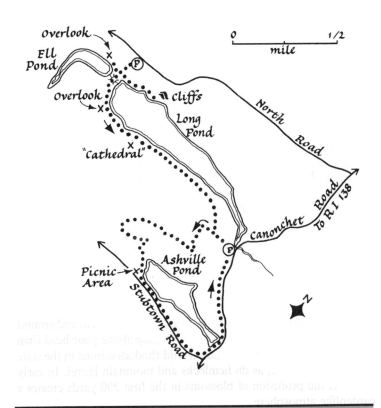

THIS WALK IS THROUGH A FOREST NOW CALLED
the Long Pond-Ell Pond Natural Area, and outstanding natural
features are just what you will find. The first section is so spectacular
it might be called the "magnificent mile."

In addition to Long Pond and Ell Pond, you will visit Ashville
Pond — a full circuit runs about 4½ miles and will take you 3
hours or more. The path is the southern terminus of the Appalachian
Mountain Club's (AMC) Narragansett Trail (see Walk 9), which
also goes into Connecticut.

Included on the fairly strenuous walk are climbs up rocky overlooks above the ponds, a descent through a deep gorge, pauses
beneath towering rhododendrons and hemlocks, and a look at several unusual rock formations, among them a cathedral-like setting
back in the woods.

In 1974, this area was entered in the Registry of Natural Land-
marks, because the site "possesses exceptional value as an illustration
of the nation's natural heritage and contributes to a better under-
standing of man's environment." A plaque stating as much had
been embedded in a boulder above Ell Pond but vanished a few
years ago.

ACCESS

To reach the start of this walk, follow RI 138 to the Hopkinton
village of Rockville, near the Connecticut border. Pick up Canonchet
Road, turn south, and drive ½ mile to North Road. Proceed right
on North Road for 1 mile (after ½ mile the roadway becomes gravel)
and park off the road on the left, where you see an AMC sign and
the yellow blazes for the trail. There is also a parking lot another
½ mile south on Canonchet Road, but the North Road access is
closer to the region's best sights.

TRAIL

Almost immediately you will be scrambling up, down, and around
boulders, but you are more apt to be looking above your head than
under your feet. Some of the tallest wild rhododendrons in the state
shade the trail here, as do hemlocks and mountain laurel. In early
summer, the profusion of blossoms in the first 200 yards creates a
gardenlike atmosphere.

Remember, however, that this is not a walk for those out of shape. By the time you reach the high bluffs above Ell Pond and Long Pond, less than ¼ mile from the start, you are likely to be huffing and puffing, and the climbs get tougher on the far side of the ponds. After struggling up a huge, angular rock mass, you reach an intersection. The yellow-blazed trail plunges straight ahead — and straight down — through the gorge. Side paths break off to the left and right and both are worth exploring before venturing into the gorge.

To the right, you emerge on a bluff overlooking Ell Pond. The shallow, L-shaped bog, one of Rhode Island's few true bogs, is nearly 70 feet below you. The vista is likely to make you linger.

The cutoff to the left from the main trail winds around to another series of high bluffs, this time facing Long Pond. Once, these rocks were a gathering place in warmer months for young people, who partied here while diving off the lower cliffs into the pond and left behind beer cans and broken bottles. The bluffs are considerably cleaner now that the area is patrolled by a state ranger. Ownership of property around the ponds is shared by the state, the Nature Conservancy, and the Audubon Society of Rhode Island.

Back on the yellow trail, ease yourself down into the gorge. It is steep and narrow, but an AMC work force recently rearranged some of the rocks and now the descent is much easier, almost a stairway. On both sides, solid walls of stone tower above you.

You round a bend at the bottom of the cleft and cross a bridge over a brook that links the two ponds. The trail then curves left along a steep slope, then winds through numerous strenuous drops and rises toward Long Pond. Twice you emerge on rocky overlooks that provide excellent views across the water to the high bluffs you visited earlier.

Also, you climb through the rocky area I call the "cathedral." You enter through an archway of rhododendrons. The ceiling is dense hemlock, so thick the "room" is permanently dimmed. Huge rocks jumbled across the steep slope represent the pews. You pick your way up the narrow aisles until the trail leaves the hemlocks. As you pass through here, you may find yourself speaking in hushed, reverent tones. I often do.

There is more up-and-down going beyond the cathedral, until you see a tumbledown stone wall. For the next several hundred yards, you follow the wall atop a stony ridge, high above the narrow

35

pond. When you finally turn right, away from the pond, you are near a short side trail to the left that takes you to the Canonchet Road parking lot. The yellow-blazed trail, however, swings abruptly right, then left, for the walk to Ashville Pond.

It is 1 mile from here to Ashville Pond, though the walking is considerably easier than in the first mile stretch. For much of the way, you are walking through thickets of mountain laurel. It is an easier if less spectacular segment than the blossomed area around Ell Pond.

The trail ends at picturesque Ashville Pond in a picnic area, where there is a shelter and outhouses. I prefer returning by taking the paved road, Stubtown Road, left to Canonchet Road (to the right, Stubtown ends at a landfill), then going left again past the other side of Ashville Pond and rejoining the yellow trail at the Canonchet parking lot. By road, the walk is slightly longer but also faster, and it avoids having to retrace your entire hike.

From the Canonchet parking lot, you will have to rewalk the ridges and gorges around Long and Ell ponds to your car, but it is only 1 magnificent mile.

9. Narragansett Trail

A walk through thickets of laurel, over rock ledges and numerous brooks, to a spectacular ravine

Hiking distance: 4 miles
Hiking time: 2 hours

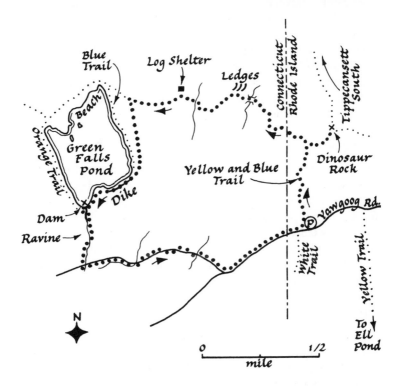

WALKING THIS SECTION OF THE NARRAGANSETT
Trail in Hopkinton has changed some in recent years, but it still provides splendid scenery as well as plenty of exercise.

Because of problems involved in crossing Boy Scout property on the west side of Yawgoog Pond, the recommended route has been shortened considerably and restricted to the north side of Yawgoog Road. Consequently, while the walk begins and ends in Rhode Island, most of it is in Connecticut, including a visit to the picturesque Green Falls Pond and its magnificent ravine. With hikers, state lines are not important.

Now a 4-mile walk, this route also rambles through immense thickets of mountain laurel, climbs numerous rock ledges, crosses gurgling brooks, and swings by a log shelter before ending with a walk along a gravel road. In addition, it hooks up with Tippecansett South (Walk 10), so you have an option of lengthening the hike.

The yellow-blazed Narragansett Trail, devised by the Appalachian Mountain Club, still runs around the western side of Yawgoog Pond to the Long Pond-Ell Pond Natural Area (Walk 8), but at this writing there is talk of rerouting the path to avoid conflicts with Boy Scout trails. A check with the Yawgoog Boy Scout Camp or a hiking club is advised before walking that path.

ACCESS

To reach the start of this walk, drive RI 138 west of Rockville a short distance to Yawgoog Road. Follow the paved road to the entrance of the scout camp, then take the gravel road to the right for 1.2 miles, parking on a wide shoulder near an upright stone that shows faded blue and yellow paint. You will pass other blazed paths before reaching this point, including the yellow trail going left, and a white-blazed trail directly across from your start. Most of these paths are for scouts only.

TRAIL

Head into the woods on the right on a trail marked in blue discs, light blue paint, and yellow paint. You are very close to the state line; blue paint refers to the AMC's Connecticut trail system and the yellow is for Rhode Island.

This section of trail is not used as much as in past years, and the trail is narrow, with bushes crowding in from both sides. Many of the bushes are laurel, and the blossom show is spectacular in June. In less than ½ mile, the trail forks. Go to the right. You'll soon find yourself scrambling up and down ledges and outcroppings, and there will be no more blue discs. Arrow signs on trees will show the way to the Tippecansett Trail. Even if you do not intend to walk that trail, go a few yards on the connector path. It crosses a narrow valley and then climbs a massive stone ridge called Dinosaur Rock. This is the southern terminus of our Tippecansett South walk, although the Tippecansett Trail itself goes east through the woods out to Yawgoog Road.

When back at the trail junction, take the yellow-and-blue Narragansett as it climbs over boulders and ledges. Soon the blazes are all blue, indicating you are in Connecticut. You will cross, on a two-plank bridge, a rushing little stream that divides two ledges and there are numerous other delights for the rock-scramblers.

When you near another brook, the trail curves right, following the stream briefly, then crosses it near the remains of a stone foundation. Just beyond the water is a clearing dominated by a three-sided log shelter used by overnight campers. Downhill, to the left, is an outhouse. Look for a trail between the shelter and the outhouse. It is more open and shows more use than the paths walked earlier.

In minutes, you emerge on a grassy lane. You are now near Green Falls Pond. The blue blazes go right, swinging around to the water's edge where they meet an orange-blazed path coming from the opposite direction. You have three choices: follow the grassy lane left, take the blue path to the water's edge and then turn left, or circle the pond on the orange trail, passing a beach and picnic area.

By going left on the grassy lane, you quickly reach an earthen dike built along the lower end of the pond. On the left side is a stone retaining wall and on the right is a row of laurel and other bushes at the water's edge. The dike offers good views of the pond, its rocky islands and the forested shores.

At the far end of the dike, pick up the blue blazes again and take the path that follows the shoreline into a grove of hemlocks. Soon you start seeing orange marks with the blue, and the path drops down a slope to a narrow dam. If you look to the right while crossing the dam, you see a shallow pond lapping placidly at your feet. But if you look to your left, you see tops of trees, for just below the dam is a deep ravine. At the far end of the dam is a spillway and the water cascading down the rock wall creates a spraying waterfall unique to this region.

Just beyond the dam, which is far more impressive from below, the blue-blazed path plunges into the ravine, almost immediately crossing the stream on large rocks. The path runs along the water for the length of the ravine, eventually crossing the brook a second time. More intriguing than the stream, however, are the high rock walls that tower above you on both sides. Covered with moss and lichens, and permanently shaded by the dense hemlocks, these walls are green, dark, and forbidding.

When you reach a gravel road (the same road on which you parked, although in Connecticut it is called Green Falls Road), turn left. It is a mile stroll back to your car, a most pleasant mile. The seldom-used road runs through dense hemlock groves and laurel thickets.

10. Tippecansett South

A trail through the southern portion of Arcadia Management Area to Dinosaur Rock

Hiking distance: 7¼ miles
Hiking time: 3-3½ hours

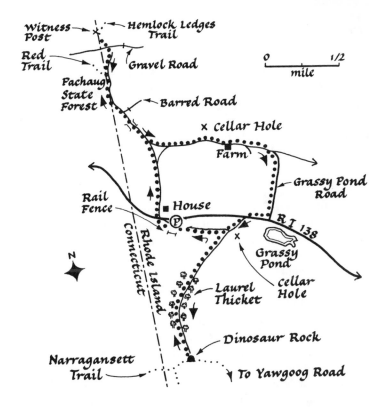

Witness Post

Hemlock Ledges Trail

Red Trail

Gravel Road

Pachaug State Forest

Barred Road

x Cellar Hole

Farm

Grassy Pond Road

Rail Fence

■ House

ℙ

R I 138

x

Grassy Pond

Rhode Island Connecticut

Laurel Thicket

Cellar Hole

N

Dinosaur Rock

Narragansett Trail

To Yawgoog Road

0   1/2
       mile

AT ITS NORTHERN END, YOU WALK THROUGH

imposing pine and hemlock forests. At its southern end, you can enjoy dense laurel and rhododendron thickets. These diverse surroundings are part of the attraction of Tippecansett South, the southern part of the long Tippecansett Trail through the Arcadia Management Area.

This trail links two of Rhode Island's most popular walking places along the western border, the Beach Pond area by way of Hemlock Ledges Trail (see Walk 11) and the Yawgoog Pond and Ell Pond region via Narragansett Trail (Walk 9). It also connects the two natural zones divided by RI 138. On this walk, you can stroll by a tranquil farm, visit two abandoned cellar holes and a massive stone ridge called Dinosaur Rock, and listen to countless birds.

ACCESS

RI 138 makes a convenient starting place with approximately 60 percent of this 7¼-mile walk on the north side of the highway and 40 percent on the south. The trail crosses the highway in Hopkinton, at a curve 5.5 miles west of I-95 (Exit 3) and 1.5 miles west of Rockville village. Leave your car at a parking area on the left. You could go into the woods from here, but for this walk begin by crossing the road, heading north.

TRAIL

The yellow-blazed trail follows a gravel driveway, past a sign denoting Noah's Ark Farm and then past a house. The gravel quickly gives way to dirt and grass but the trail continues along the route of the old road. You will pass a side road on the left and then two going to the right. You will return later to the second of these old, grassy byways for a loop around the farm, but for now continue straight ahead with the blazes.

The walking is slightly uphill, but the lane is smooth and easy. Shortly, you reach another fork. This time, bear right. Within minutes, you cross a wooden bridge and begin a steeper ascent. The trail becomes more sandy and you will notice more boulders and bedrock in the forest. As you climb, a depression appears just left of the lane and you soon find yourself on the edge of a deep ravine.

Beyond the bridge, about 1 mile from your start, you reach a roadway lined with stone walls going to the right. This road is barred and posted, so continue on the sandy road as it swings left.

You will be virtually straddling the state line at this point, sometimes a few feet in Connecticut, sometimes returning to Rhode Island. The observant may find a stone marker, on the right, with C chiseled into one side and RI on the other.

On the Connecticut side (left), you will see a stand of tall pines in which some logging recently has been done. On the right, surging undergrowth is reclaiming what once was farmland. This is prime wildlife habitat and it is not unusual to find deer tracks or grouse dusting wallows on the sandy lane.

At one of the cutover areas, you can see a trail blazed in red and blue coming in from the left. This path runs around the Connecticut side of Beach Pond. The yellow trail stays on the lane until you reach a gravel road — the southern terminus of the Hemlock Ledges segment of the Tippecansett Trail. You can continue following the trail into the woods; it emerges on RI 165 just east of Beach Pond.

For this walk, however, go only a few yards into the woods, until finding the witness post that serves as the state boundary marker, then retrace your route back down the lane, past the barred road and the wooden bridge. In slightly more than a mile from the point of your turnaround, you reach the grassy cutoff trail, now on your left. Take this lane.

At first, you stroll downhill through a dense forest, then climb briefly. When the trail levels off and opens slightly, look for a cellar hole and the remains of a huge stone fireplace and chimney on the left. Behind the house foundation is a hand-dug, stone-lined well covered by a large, rectangular rock. The well is a work of art and is worth examining, but be extremely careful; old wells often are hazardous.

Beyond the cellar hole, the trail narrows but soon opens once more. It then runs along one of the overgrown pastures of the farm, following fences and stone walls as it curls gradually to the right. You pass another pasture and then an orchard before reaching the farm buildings, where the grassy lane becomes a gravel road. You can frequently hear roosters crowing and songbirds singing in the barnyard.

For the next mile or so, you follow the roadway, turning right at the first fork. Throughout this section, you are walking between

dense forests, and in spring you can listen to a plethora of birds —
thrashers, thrushes, orioles, warblers, catbirds, towhees, vireos,
and wrens.

When you reach a paved road, you are back on RI 138. A right
turn and walk of less than ½ mile would take you back to your car.
However, you have not seen the best laurel thickets or Dinosaur
Rock yet, so take the highway to the right only as far as the first
(unblazed) lane entering the woods on the left. A short walk on this
narrow, stone-walled lane returns you to the yellow blazes of Tippecansett, rejoining the trail at a sharp turn beside a cellar hole.

Go left on the marked trail. It is 1 mile through grand thickets
of laurel — awesome in early June — to the immense outcropping
where your path joins the Narragansett Trail.

Technically, Tippecansett Trail does not end here — it swings
left from the rock and runs through more woods out to Yawgoog
Road. But your car is back on RI 138, so pause a few minutes and
look over the smooth ledge. Just why is has been called Dinosaur
Rock is unclear, but it is an impressive sight.

Return to your car by rewalking the path through the laurel and
turning left beside the cellar hole. Running along part of this final
segment is an old-fashioned, zigzagging rail fence. Such fences are
now rare in rural Rhode Island and this one is collapsing in places,
but it still represents one more link to the past. It is a fitting conclu-
sion to this walk.

11. Hemlock Ledges

Unique formations of glacial ledges and unusually picturesque hemlocks in this middle section of the Tippecansett Trail

Hiking distance: 3½ miles
Hiking time: 2 hours

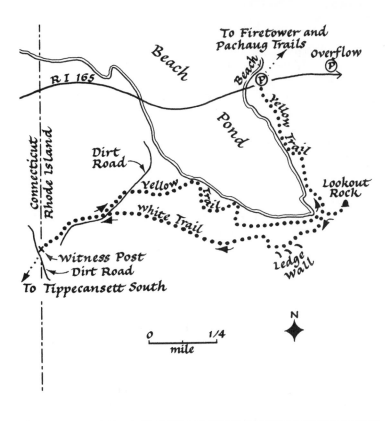

To Firetower and Pachaug Trails

Overflow

R I 165

Beach

Beach

Pond

Yellow Trail

Connecticut

Rhode Island

Dirt Road

Yellow Trail

White Trail

Lookout Rock

Witness Post

Dirt Road

To Tippecansett South

Ledge Wall

N

0   1/4
        mile

HEMLOCK LEDGES IS THE MIDDLE SEGMENT OF

the long Tippecansett Trail through the Arcadia Management Area. At one end it links with the Firetower Trail (see Walk 12) and at the other it connects with Tippecansett South (Walk 10). It is short but sweet, adding sights not readily found anywhere else along the Tippecansett.

Both the hemlock trees and the glacial ledges for which this walk is named are unusually picturesque and in this 3½-mile loop you'll see unique formations, both of trees and rocks. You will go as far as a "witness post" that marks the Connecticut border before returning to your starting point. It can be walked in less than 2 hours, but there are many interesting places where you may want to linger.

ACCESS

To reach the start of Beach Pond in Exeter, follow RI 165 west about 7 miles from I-95. The pond, which extends over the state line into Connecticut, lies at the bottom of a steep hill. There is a parking area beside the pond. If the lot is filled, as it often is during swimming season, you can find another parking area just uphill from the pond, at a former picnic area, on the right.

TRAIL

Cross the road, near the pond, to find the trail's start. It is marked with a sign saying Tippecansett and is blazed in yellow. This first section runs just back from the shoreline. On summer weekends, you are likely to find many fishermen, walkers, and children here, an overflow from the crowded beach.

Because of its heavy use, the area is laced with numerous paths and trails, so be sure to follow the yellow blazes. They will quickly lead you to a higher ridge that curves back toward the shoreline. In a matter of minutes, you are away from the crowds and among the hemlocks and ledges. Several times, the path crosses boulders that offer excellent views of the shallow pond, which, in summer, is decorated with blooming lilies and an abundance of bird life.

Near the end of the pond, the trail turns left into a dense hemlock grove and begins climbing. When you reach a fork, 0.7 mile from your start, you are close to the most impressive ledges in the area. The yellow trail goes downhill to the right, a white-blazed path runs straight ahead, and another white-marked path goes up a steep

46

slope to the left, crossing a rock with the notation "LOOKOUT" in faded yellow paint.

Take the left turn to the lookout first. In a few strides, you are at the base of a high bluff. The path edges to the right and then claws its way up through a crevice. In minutes you are standing atop the highest spot in the area. This roundish outcrop enables you to see across Beach Pond to the woods and cottages on the Connecticut side far beyond. For many hikers, this vista is their reason for walking Hemlock Ledges and they often return to their cars after pausing here.

To continue the loop to the witness post, however, return to the junction and take the unnamed white-blazed path, now on your left. Soon you will reach another white-marked trail with a sign saying Deep Pond Trail going off to your left. The word CONN. and an arrow painted on a tree will keep you on the correct route.

A virtual wall of glacial rock lines the left side of this section for some distance, and you should take your time here, inspecting the trees — most of them hemlocks — that are growing out of cracks and crevices in the ledges. Many are quite old and large, and protrude from what appears to be solid rock.

The trail continues following the wall until its end, then swings abruptly to the right and curls upward over rocky terrain. Now, you are walking through an open forest. The hemlocks are fewer in number but more impressive in size, with several magnificent, tall, straight giants. The understory here includes thickets of mountain laurel, which are spectacular when blooming in late spring and green throughout the rest of the year.

When you reach a dirt road, you are at the end of the white-blazed trail. The yellow trail follows the road here. Turn left, walk a short distance, and watch for the path off the road, to the right, back into the forest of young oaks and blueberry bushes. Within minutes, you will reach the metal sign, the witness post mentioned earlier. It stands beside a survey marker embedded in rock: the state boundary.

If you walk a few more feet, you reach a second dirt road and the northern terminus of the Tippecansett South Trail (see Walk 10). For the Hemlock Ledges walk, however, turn around and recross the narrow woodlot back to the first dirt road. Follow the yellow blazes beyond the trail you walked earlier and reenter the woods, farther downhill, on the right.

This route takes you through more dense laurel thickets as it winds its way back toward the pond. As you near the water, you return to hemlock stands and boulders, and both the trees and the rocks increase in size as you gradually climb back toward the crossroads near Lookout Rock. Again, there are many side trails that run to the water's edge. When you reach the junction, go left for the return to your car.

12. Firetower Trail

A car-shuttle walk from Beach Pond to the inspiring Stepstone Falls

Hiking distance: 3¾ miles
Hiking time: 2 hours

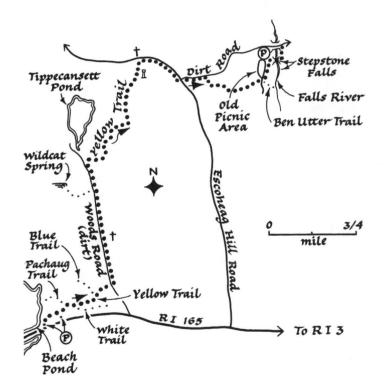

SAVE THIS WALK FOR AN AUTUMN MORNING. Pick a cool, crisp day when the leaves have turned color, and you are in for a treat.

Firetower Trail runs between two lovely spots, Beach Pond and Stepstone Falls. It is the northern end of the long Tippecansett Trail maintained by the Appalachian Mountain Club, and is relatively short, just 3¾ miles. However, because it links with other trails at both ends, the ambitious can easily extend the walk if they wish. This is not a walk to hurry through, though; take your time and enjoy the autumn forest.

Do not plan this walk for late November or early December — deer hunting season. A mile section in the middle of this route is closed to walkers during that time.

You will be in woods virtually all the way. The first section is an easy stroll along old roadways, then there is a rocky but delightful segment, and you end with a downhill ramble through a pine grove. Along the way, you pass two old cemeteries, numerous stone walls marching through the woods, a spring, a pond, an abandoned field filled with blueberry bushes, and the firetower for which this walk is named.

ACCESS

For a one-way walk, you will need to place a car at Stepstone Falls. Drive RI 165 west from RI 3 and I-95 about 5 miles to Escoheag Hill Road. Turn right and proceed about 2½ miles to an unmarked dirt road (you will see double yellow blazes on a electrical pole at the corner). Go right and follow the winding, rutted old road downhill until reaching a concrete bridge. There is room to park on the right. The falls, also reached by the Ben Utter Trail (Walk 17), are just a few yards downstream, to the right.

To reach the trail's start, go back south on Escoheag Hill Road to RI 165, turn right and drive about 2 miles to Beach Pond, which straddles the state line. You can park at the beach — there is usually plenty of room in autumn — and pick up the trail where it crosses the highway. The Tippecansett segment on the south side of the highway is known as the Hemlock Ledges Trail (see Walk 11).

TRAIL

At the start, the yellow blazes for the Firetower Trail run along

50

with the blue marks for the Pachaug Trail (Walk 13) for a short distance, going uphill from Beach Pond, through the back of an abandoned picnic grove, and then turning left and dropping down a slope. As soon as they cross a dirt road, the trails divide, the Pachaug going to the left and the Firetower going right on a grassy lane.

It is time to start enjoying the scenery. Maples, brilliant in autumn, glow overhead. Birches, beeches, oaks, and ashes add colorful variety. The lane runs gradually uphill but is easy to walk. Early in this segment you will pass a white-blazed trail going off to the right and then a blue-blazed path going left. Stay with the yellow marks.

About ¾ mile from the start, the trail turns left on a wider woods road that is maintained as a fire lane. Stone walls run along both sides of the road in places and many other walls can be seen in the forest. A short distance along this road, you will pass, on the right, a family cemetery guarded by a splendid stone wall and iron gate. Most of the headstones date from the 1800s.

The next landmark, about ¼ mile beyond the cemetery, is a white-blazed side path to the left and a sign pointing the way to Wildcat Spring. This is a pleasant little detour, a winding walk downhill to the spring, which bubbles out of a jumble of rocks at the base of a huge maple. It runs more freely in April and May than autumn but is worth a look at any time. A visit to the spring and the walk back will add about ⅓ mile to your hike.

Back on the yellow trail, you soon reach a sharp turn right, marked by double blazes and an arrow sign. You are nearly to Tippecansett Pond but because of thick brush the water is hidden from view.

You will pass a sign indicating you are entering private property and that walking is prohibited during deer season. This section of the walk is through surging new growth — bushes, vines and small trees — that has taken over since a logging operation a few years ago. The trail is not hard to follow, but some care is necessary where there are side paths. In most cases, blazes are painted on rocks.

When you reach an area with taller trees, you may be able to glimpse the pond through the forest on your left, but you never get good views. You will cross a sparkling brook on a pile of rocks, just below a dam made of rocks, then go uphill through a grove of taller trees.

In an area more recently logged, watch for the second sign about deer season. Almost beneath the sign, just beyond a tiny brook, the trail takes a sharp turn left off the logging road. Be careful; the cutoff is easy to miss.

This is a particularly inviting section. Beech trees add a golden glow over a rocky terrain. The path is less worn here but not difficult to follow as it snakes its way uphill over small ledges and ridges. Then, suddenly, you emerge from the woods at the foot of the tall firetower, which is fenced and locked.

Proceed past the tower to the paved road (Escoheag Hill Road). Take a moment to look over a well-kept cemetery directly across the road, then turn right and follow the pavement around a bend. Watch for the blazes on a pole beside the dirt road. Turn left on this dirt road, and you are on your final leg of the walk.

You can follow the road all the way to your car, but the marked trail soon turns right, through an opening in a stone wall, into an abandoned field. It curls left, running parallel to the road briefly, then gradually swings right as it wanders downhill. This is the blueberry thicket that makes many walkers linger in July.

Beyond the field, the trail goes through a pine grove before ending on a junction of two paved but abandoned roads in the old Stepstone Falls Picnic Area, which is no longer accessible by car. The yellow blazes continue, but now are part of the Ben Utter Trail, heading to the right, following the Falls River downstream.

To reach the falls and your car, leave all blazes behind and go left on the lower road past a pumphouse and an outhouse. Turn right on a grassy lane that soon becomes a well-worn path running around the end of a stone wall. It goes down stone steps to a T intersection with another path. Go left, still downhill, and you will soon hear the falls.

When you reach a white-blazed trail, you have a choice. Straight ahead is one of the finer portions of the falls; water drops down the flat stones as if going from shelf to shelf, or step to step. To the left is your car, but to the right is the footbridge that runs over another part of the falls.

It's a beautiful spot, and once very popular. Now, with the picnic grounds closed, it is far more secluded but still as lovely as ever. For the best views of the falls, take the white-marked trail along the shore to the bridge, cross the stream and return on the opposite side. The path will return across the concrete bridge and deliver you directly to your car.

13. Pachaug Trail

A strenuous walk past glacial boulders and sheer cliffs through wild terrain virtually untouched since its formation

Hiking distance: 8 miles
Hiking time: 3½-4 hours

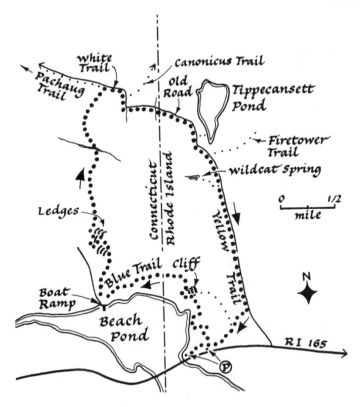

BUILD UP TO THIS WALK. TRY SOME OF THE
shorter and easier trails first. The Pachaug will test your muscles
and stamina. It's long, just over 8 miles, and the first 5 miles are
among the most strenuous segments in this book. But it's a fun
walk and a beautiful one. You climb over rugged ledges, scrambling
up and down ravines and chasms, in the first part, then finish up
with a few miles on flat old woods lanes.

This route is actually parts of three hiking trails and runs a mile
or more on an unmarked lane. You start in Rhode Island, swing
around a pond into Connecticut, then return to Rhode Island past
another pond and a spring.

ACCESS

To start, drive RI 165 about 7 miles west of RI 3 and I-95 to
Beach Pond, which straddles the state line. You can park beside
the pond unless it's summer and the beach lot is filled. In summer,
retreat up the hill along RI 165 a short distance to a parking area
in what was a picnic area. The Pachaug starts at the beach but runs
along the back of the old picnic grounds so you can start at either
place.

TRAIL

The Pachaug is blazed in blue but you also will see yellow blazes
for the long Tippecansett Trail. The paths run together at first, and
you will be returning on the Tippecansett, which in this area is
often called the Firetower Trail (see Walk 12).

Follow the blue and yellow blazes (from the beach or the picnic
grove) as they run east, parallel to the highway, for a short distance.
The trails then turn left, drop down a slope, and cross a dirt road
before splitting. Stay with the blue trail.

The Pachaug Trail runs back toward Beach Pond, twice going
all the way to the shoreline, before making a curl around the pond's
eastern side. You will quickly get an idea of the terrain, as the trail
is rocky and hilly. And it keeps getting rockier and hillier.

If the going appears too difficult, you have an option. About a
mile from the start, you reach a cutoff trail, on the right, that runs
through the woods to the Firetower Trail. If you stay on the blue

trail, you will now be going west around Beach Pond, soon passing a small blue sign that indicates you are crossing the state line.

Hemlocks and glacial boulders dominate this area and the next few miles. The huge, angular rocks, many of them green with coverings of moss and lichens, are scattered about and the trail seems to visit the largest and most picturesque. At times, you walk at the base of sheer cliffs. Other times, you pick your way up narrow clefts and around vertical ledges.

For nearly a mile, this rock-scrambling goes on. Gradually, you work your way down a slope. When you emerge on a dirt road, you are near the pond once more. Cross the road (which is private) and follow the path as it runs to the shoreline, then turns right. In minutes, you are at a public boat ramp.

From the ramp, cross the parking area and pick up the trail again in bushes to the right of the roadway. The path immediately goes back up and over rocky ridges. You soon cross a dirt lane and then the trail levels off briefly.

Just as you begin thinking the toughest part is past, however, the path suddenly swings left and drops down a deep chasm. Now you are entering the most strenuous, but also most impressive, section. Up and around, over and down, the trail snakes through ravines, climbs ledges and bounces over boulders. This is wild terrain, virtually untouched since formed by the glaciers. The dense canopy of the hemlocks keeps the ground in permanent shade and there is little underbrush. Tiny red squirrels are common and birds can be heard overhead, but the area has an eerie, intriguing aura found along few other hikes in this book. It is certainly worth the effort.

Eventually, the trail starts climbing and curves gently to the right, finally leaving the hemlocks and entering the area of laurel, hardwoods, and stone walls. You cross a woods road and then head slightly downhill through a cutover area where the surging new bushes have all but obliterated the trail. This is the most tricky section of the walk, as far as following the blazes is concerned, but with care you can follow the footpath until it returns to taller trees.

When you reach a gravel lane, at about 5 miles, look for a sign for the Canonicus Trail, blazed in white, pointing right. Take it, leaving the Pachaug and its blue blazes, which turn left.

Follow the Canonicus only a short distance, rounding a bend in the road. At the second bend, the trail turns left, into the woods (it ends at the firetower of Firetower Trail). Instead, stay on the gravel road, which is most pleasant to walk with tall trees and stone walls on both sides and plenty of ferns and other undergrowth.

Ignore the numerous lanes running off the road, which makes a sharp turn left and passes an area where there has been some recent logging. Eventually, the gravel gives way to dirt and the roadway narrows, but at all times it remains wide enough to be used as a fire lane. It is shortly after leaving the gravel that you recross the line back into Rhode Island.

You are now walking around the western side of Tippecansett Pond, but there are few views of the shallow pond because of the trees. The land on the left, next to the pond, is posted, but there is one cutoff lane running to the water that offers a look.

Shortly after passing this cutoff, you will notice the yellow blazes of the Tippecansett (Firetower) Trail turning from this road off into the brush on the left. For the remainder of this walk, you will be following the yellow blazes back toward Beach Pond.

Soon after joining the yellow trail, you will pass a white-marked path to the right with a sign pointing toward Wildcat Spring. For a description of the spring, see Walk 12. A detour to the spring and back would add about one-third of a mile to your walk.

The yellow blazes take you along the woods road more than half a mile, then turn right and follow a narrower lane west. Along this lane, you pass the blue connector trail that runs to the Pachaug, then finally you reach the spot where the yellow and blue trails originally split. A left turn and a climb up the slope takes you to the old picnic grove. Beach Pond is just a short distance farther. After this walk, a refreshing dip in the cool waters may be needed more than a lunch.

14. Escoheag Trail

A gradual descent through state-owned forest to natural and man-made waterfalls

Hiking distance: 3 miles
Hiking time: 2 hours

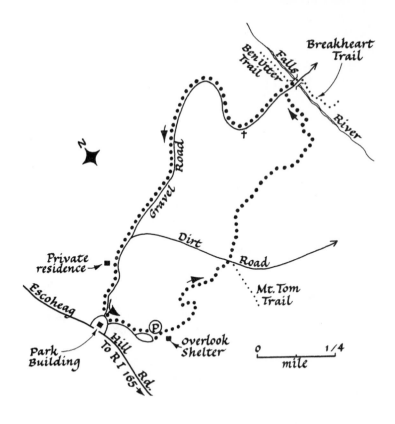

ESCOHEAG TRAIL IS A PLEASANT, EASY-TO-WALK path on its own, but it can serve equally well as a warm-up for hikes to a couple of Rhode Island's best wild places.

The 3-mile loop described here wanders mostly downhill through a state-owned forest, then returns along an unpaved woods road. At the far end of the loop, the ambitious can easily extend the walk by going up to Penny Hill on the Breakheart Trail (see Walk 16) or by following a stream to Stepstone Falls on the Ben Utter Trail (Walk 17).

ACCESS

To reach the start of Escoheag, take RI 165 west about 5½ miles from RI 3, turn right on Escoheag Hill Road, and continue for 1 mile. Turn right on a gravel road next to a log building. This is the old Beach Pond State Recreation Area, now largely unused except by hikers, horsemen, trail bikers, and, in season, hunters. Turn right again in just a few yards on a narrow lane leading back to a circular drive in what was a picnic area. Park your car here. The white blazes that mark the start of the trail are easy to see at the far end of the loop.

TRAIL

You begin by dropping down a rocky slope, but in minutes you will see a side trail going right, up to the top of a large outcropping. It is worth the time and effort to make the climb, for at the very edge of the ledge is a stone-sided shelter, another leftover from the area's days as a popular place for weekend outings. This spot gave the area its name — the Ledges Picnic Area. It is seldom used for picnics now, but in winter and after the leaves have dropped in fall, it is an excellent place to look over the surrounding woodlands.

From the shelter, an unmarked trail winds around the ledge down to the main hiking trail. Almost immediately, you see that walkers share this path with bikers, and in several spots the bikers have created side paths around wet places, ledges, or other obstacles. Be careful to stay on the white-marked path.

You also will have to look carefully after you skirt the bottom of a large outcropping and climb to the flat top. The trail crosses the table rock and reenters the woods at the extreme left.

This climb is one of the few you will have to make; most of the walk is a gradual downhill stroll. There are numerous little brooks to cross (a great number of them in spring and after heavy rains), but for the most part it is an easy walk. Small beech trees and scattered thickets of laurel make the woods attractive even in late fall and winter.

In less than 1 mile from your start, you will emerge on a dirt road. Just to your right, you will see blazes and a sign for the Mount Tom Trail (see Walk 18) coming in from RI 165. Mount Tom walkers either continue on the Escoheag Trail or turn right here and follow the old road back to their cars.

Escoheag Trail continues across the dirt road and runs mostly downhill. The walking is easy at first, but gradually returns to rocky terrain similar to the area near your start. There are no ledges to climb, however, and you can proceed quite rapidly and comfortably.

When the trail reaches a grove of pine trees, you are near the river that is your goal. The path swings abruptly left on an overgrown lane and runs out to a sandy road. This is the road you will walk back, to the left, but first take a few moments to go right to the river.

Just before the river, on the left side of the road, is a sign indicating the start of the Ben Utter Trail, which leads to Stepstone Falls. A walk to the falls and back, following the white blazes, would add only about 2½ miles to your hike. Across the bridge, on the right, is the start of the Breakheart Trail. If you take it up to Penny Hill and back, following the yellow blazes, you will walk an additional 1¼ miles or so.

Even if you take neither extension, a visit to the rushing stream, called Falls River, is a pleasant diversion. It is a clear, noisy stream that features natural and man-made waterfalls. They make the place attractive in all seasons.

As you start your return up the road, you may notice a metal sign indicating a historical cemetery off in the woods on the left. The graveyard is not easy to find — it's nearly 100 yards back in the forest, on a small knoll — but is interesting. The small, ancient tombstones are weathered and illegible, for the most part, but one is accompanied by a rusted metal marker placed by the Society of Sons of the American Revolution. It is a most peaceful final resting place.

The road you return on is barred to automobiles much of the

year but is open in hunting season. You are likely, however, to find horsemen on the road virtually any time of the year. The walk is relatively easy, though the grade is quite steep where the road makes a horseshoe bend around to the right. Forest crowds in on both sides and numerous seasonal brooks trickle underneath.

You will pass a dirt road going to the left (the same road you crossed at the end of the Mount Tom Trail) and then a residence on the right. There is another barway here that regulates traffic on the road.

In moments, you are at the old park entrance, and a walk down the lane to the left returns you to your car.

15. Frosty Hollow

A winding stroll to Penny Hill through pine forests, over brooks, and through thickets of mountain laurel

Hiking distance: 7 miles
Hiking time: 3 hours

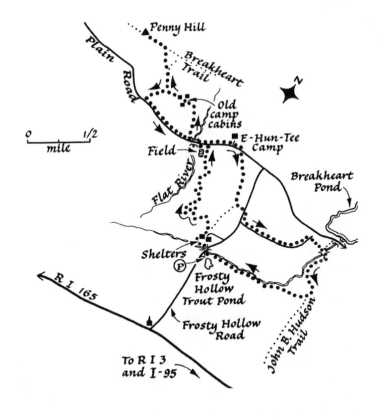

IF YOU LIKE WOODS WALKING, AND ARE IN NO hurry to get anywhere in particular, Frosty Hollow is your trail. It wanders around in an erratic manner and ends where it began, but it can be a thoroughly enjoyable walk.

Still another hike in the Arcadia Management Area, this route is actually parts of three established paths. It goes from a trout pond, past a small camping area, through a delightful pine forest, crosses a stream, runs through an abandoned complex of cabins, then climbs to Penny Hill.

That's only the first half of this walk. You then recross the stream, walk along a dirt road, swing through more woods, including a park-like segment, follow a picturesque brook in thickets of mountain laurel, and finish up on an easy-to-walk lane.

This route is 7 miles long, but there are several optional cutoffs that would reduce the distance.

ACCESS

To reach the starting point, take RI 165 west from RI 3 about 3 miles to Frosty Hollow Road, then turn right at the West Exeter Church. In less than 1 mile, you reach Frosty Hollow Trout Pond, on your right. Park in the small lot between the pond and a stream, and look for the white blazes at the bridge that crosses the stream.

TRAIL

Technically, the path marked in white is called the Shelter Trail, but because that name is unimaginative and this route also overlaps two yellow-blazed trails, the Breakheart (see Walk 16) and John B. Hudson (Walk 19) trails, many walkers have taken to using the more lyrical Frosty Hollow name of both the gravel road and the trout pond.

Begin by crossing the road bridge, then following the white blazes left into the forest. Almost immediately, the path swings right and reaches the shelters for which the trail is named. You pass through the tiny campground quickly, then turn left on a woods lane closed to vehicles. The lane is an easy, open path carpeted in pine needles. In spring, you will find violets, ladyslippers, bluets, and buttercups blooming, and you likely will be accompanied by numerous forest birds, particularly thrushes, wrens, and tanagers.

After the lane passes a stone wall and starts curving downhill to the right, look for a sharp cutoff to the left. The trail now becomes quite narrow and wanders back and forth for about a mile through a mixed woods dominated by tall pines. Eventually, you find yourself on another old lane that ends at a barway beside an open field.

The trail runs beside a line of pines past the field to a sandy road, known locally as Plain Road. Go left a short distance, cross a bridge, then turn right into the woods. Once again, you begin on an old lane that narrows to a footpath. When you reach a well-used motorbike trail, turn left.

You climb up a rather steep slope and suddenly emerge amid several small cabins, part of the abandoned Beach Pond Camps complex. Once a bustling little village in summer, it is now a place of silence. On a recent visit here, I saw a deer stroll through the yard. Take a few minutes to look over the buildings and the rusting water tower, then follow the gravel lane that leads away from the buildings. You can follow the lane out to Plain Road, but the white trail takes a sharp right and reenters the forest.

When the trail splits, take the less-worn left fork. (The right fork also goes to Breakheart Trail and you could then turn right and

Abandoned cabins of an old campground suddenly appear in the forest along the Frosty Hollow walk.

eventually reach Breakheart Pond.) The left fork runs through a boulder-strewn ravine, then ends at the yellow-marked Breakheart Trail. A left turn and steep climbs up two slopes take you to Penny Hill, one of the highest spots in the area. This is the halfway point in your walk and an ideal place for a rest.

To resume walking, return to the white trail and retrace your route back down to the gravel road at the old camp. Turn right and follow the camp road to Plain Road. A left turn and a walk of roughly a mile on this road will take you beyond the open field where you emerged earlier. Stay on Plain Road until reaching the E-Hun-Tee camp on your left. Here, a white-blazed path goes into the forest on the right. Take this path, and follow it until reaching a tree with three trail signs. One points the way back to the shelters, a second is for the segment you just walked, and a third indicates a path going to Breakheart Pond's south end. That is the route you follow.

The trail quickly reaches Frosty Hollow Road. You can turn right and be back at your car in 0.4 mile, making a hike of approximately 6 miles. However, you would miss some of the trail's highlights, so cross the road and follow the white blazes into the woods along a barred lane.

This section has the park-like stand of tall pines, and your pace is likely to slow as you watch the warblers and vireos flitting through the boughs. The lane curves to the left and ends near a small parking area for hunters coming in from Plain Road. The path goes along the right side of the parking lot briefly, then turns right and goes through woods to a former picnic area. You can turn left here and soon be at Breakheart Pond and its distinctive fish ladder.

Or you can stay to the right, pick up the yellow blazes of the John B. Hudson Trail and cross Breakheart Brook on a footbridge. The Hudson Trail turns right after you cross the stream and runs through a glorious thicket of mountain laurel. You follow the gurgling, rocky stream for some distance, then climb to the left to higher ground.

Shortly after leaving the stream, you reach an intersection of trails. Look to the right for the sign saying Shelter Trail nailed high on a tree. Take this trail and enjoy the final section of your walk. It gradually descends toward the stream, then goes through a lovely area of laurel and pines. The trail will take you into the parking lot where your car awaits.

16. Breakheart Trail

A combination of easy and strenuous walking from Breakheart Pond to Penny Hill and back

Hiking distance: 6 miles
Hiking time: 3½-4 hours

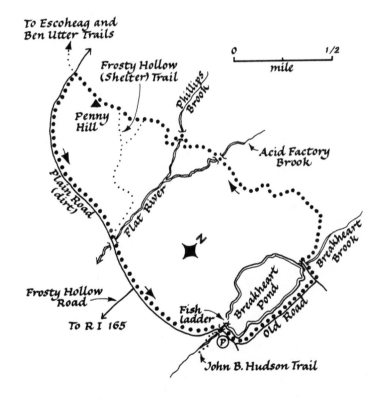

BREAKHEART POND AND PENNY HILL ARE PIC-
turesque places popular with outdoorsmen but are remote and nearly
unknown to most Rhode Islanders.

This 6-mile walk visits both places, combining an easy walk
around the pond with a more strenuous hike through dense forest
up to the hill's summit. The walk ends with a 2-mile stroll along a
little-used gravel road. Don't let this stretch on a road dissuade
you; a great many times walks along roads like this are very rewarding, particularly if you are interested in songbirds. You will see
more wildlife along roads than in dense forests, where the foliage
is too thick and the walking too noisy.

This is another walk in the state-owned Arcadia Management
Area in Exeter and West Greenwich, and the yellow-blazed trail
connects with the John B. Hudson Trail (see Walk 19) at one end
and the Ben Utter (Walk 17) and Escoheag (Walk 14) trails at the
other.

A number of the problems of a few years ago have been remedied.
Two rickety bridges over brooks far back in the forest have been
replaced, and some of the erosion problems (but not all) on steep
slopes have been repaired.

Keep in mind that this is a heavily used area in certain seasons
and you may run into fishermen, hunters, horsemen, motorcyclists,
or, as I did once, a dog-sled team. Also, there are numerous dirt
roads and lanes and pathways crisscrossing these woods, so be
careful to stay with the yellow blazes. Wandering off on side trails
could get you lost.

ACCESS

To reach Breakheart Pond, take RI 165 exactly 3 miles west of
RI 3. Turn right (north) at the West Exeter Baptist Church on
gravel Frosty Hollow Road, continue 1½ miles to its end, then go
right on another gravel road until it ends at the pond.

TRAIL

Before starting your walk, look over the dam and concrete fish
ladder beside the parking area. The fish ladder, a series of shallow,
rectangular pools, was built to help trout get over the dam and
return upstream to spawn. It is one of the few ladders of its kind

in the state. Breakheart Pond, as well as Breakheart Brook and Breakheart Road, all derive their names from nearby Breakheart Hill, which was named for the heartbreaking task of attempting to drive oxen up its slopes long ago.

To follow Breakheart Trail, swing around the right side of the pond on an open, abandoned roadway. It quickly passes a cellar hole and there are numerous stone walls, showing this was once farmland. At the far end of the pond, you'll reach another old road. You could take it completely around the pond, making an easy 1½-mile walk. The yellow trail, however, turns right, into the forest, immediately after crossing a footbridge over Breakheart Brook.

The trail soon leaves the brook and angles uphill through dense, brushy woods. There are plenty of rocks, but the footing is not difficult. As the ascent grows steeper, the path opens somewhat. Pines and oaks are the dominant trees, and the number of squirrels and chipmunks in the area increases accordingly. On one walk here, my young son counted 22 chipmunks and 12 squirrels.

Off to the right, you'll see white signs nailed to trees. This marks the boundary of the University of Rhode Island's agricultural and biological research area, called the Alton Jones Campus. No trespassing is allowed.

You'll begin crossing unmarked lanes and gravel roads. Be sure to find the yellow blazes before taking paths. At one point, the trail crosses a road and goes into a grove of very young pines, where the blazes can be difficult to find. Quickly, though, it opens onto a wider path and curls downhill, to the right, and crosses a stream called Acid Factory Brook. This bridge, approximately 2¼ miles from the start, is one of those replaced in recent years.

After some up and down going, the trail levels off through a park-like grove of tall pines, then swings left (again, be careful; another path goes straight ahead). You'll cross a second stream, Phillips Brook, on another solid bridge before heading into the most hilly section of this walk.

Here, steps have been taken to correct some of the erosion problems with logs and stones on the slopes, and in a few places the trail has been rerouted slightly to avoid some muddy areas. You'll pass a white-marked cutoff with a sign that says Shelter Trail (see Walk 15), cross a steep hill, pass a second Shelter Trail crossing, and then begin the gradual ascent up Penny Hill.

The rocky summit of Penny Hill is only 370 feet above sea level, but it is higher than the surrounding countryside and makes you feel you are much higher as you overlook the forests. It is 3.7 miles from your start, and an excellent place to pause and rest.

Going down the opposite side is easy, and in just a few minutes you emerge on a gravel road, which here is more sand than gravel. Turn left and walk. It is nearly 2 miles back to your car, but it is a very pleasant 2 miles with good footing and plenty of birds in the roadside bushes.

There are some side roads going off to the right, but stay on the main road. It gently curves left, crosses a river, and passes Camp E-Hun-Tee, a private wilderness camp for boys, back in the woods on the left. There are no other buildings along the entire 2 miles. Once you pass the camp signs, it is less than ½ mile to the finish.

17. Ben Utter Trail

A leisurely walk along a scenic river culminating at Stepstone Falls

Hiking distance: 3½ miles
Hiking time: 2 hours

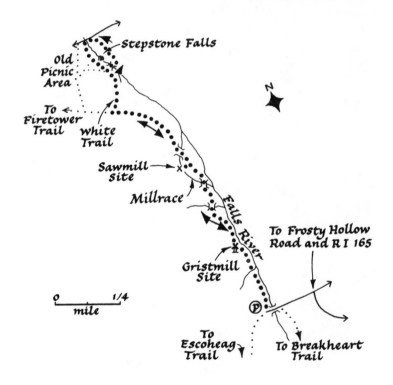

THE BEN UTTER TRAIL IS PERFECT FOR THOSE
who regard hiking as a relaxing pastime and a means of viewing
the handiwork of both nature and man rather than an athletic endurance event.

This trail, named for one of the guiding lights behind the Rhode
Island trails system, is short (about 3½ miles, round-trip), relatively
level, and very accommodating. Wooden bridges span the brooks
and stone steps ease your way up and down the steeper ridges.

Stepstone Falls is the focal point of several different trails.

Following the aptly named Falls River upstream, this trail passes the remains of an old gristmill and a sawmill, leads through thickets of mountain laurel and dense growths of ferns, and culminates at Stepstone Falls, one of Rhode Island's most beautiful spots.

The trail runs between two dirt roads in the Exeter portion of the Arcadia Management Area, and links with the Firetower Trail (see Walk 12), the Escoheag Trail (Walk 14), and the Breakheart Trail (Walk 16). Once this area was very popular, but the closing of some forest roads in recent years has made access to Stepstone Falls and a nearby picnic area difficult. This trail also is used far less than before.

ACCESS

To reach the start, take RI 165 west from RI 3 about 3 miles to Frosty Hollow Road, a gravel lane going into the forest on the right. When you reach the end of Frosty Hollow (in 1½ miles) turn left and drive for about 2 miles, then go left at the next intersection for a short distance to a stream. Park just beyond the bridge, on the right.

TRAIL

The yellow-blazed trail runs to the right along the stream. Immediately, you can hear and see the first falls, although in this section they are man-made structures — huge logs anchored at each end with rocks — installed years ago to make the stream more attractive to trout. The tumbling waters rumble constantly, adding a pleasing, soothing overtone to your walk.

The trail climbs a stone stairway over the first ridge, once part of an earthen dam built for a gristmill. Some of the mill's stone foundations lie just off the trail on the left, but more remains can be seen on the opposite side of the stream.

You momentarily break onto an old road, now used mostly by horsemen, then turn almost immediately to the right into a laurel thicket. In early June, it is glorious enough right here, amid the bouquets of pink and white blossoms, to make the walk worthwhile.

Beyond the laurel, you cross a wooden bridge over a rushing little brook that actually was dug as a millrace for a vertical sawmill powered by a waterwheel. In a few minutes, on your left, you can

71

see what remains of the mill, a rubble of huge stone slabs. Many have fallen into the water, but it is not difficult to picture the effort that went into building the mill and digging the channel through the stony ground. Another few yards takes you to a second bridge over the millrace, and off to your right, you can see part of the dam that was built in the stream to divert water to the mill.

Up to this point, you are continually within earshot of the stream, and the moods of the hurrying little river can make each walk here seem different. I've seen the stream roaring over the falls in a frothy fury, and I've seen it gurgling over in a gentle lullaby. It all depends on the season, the water level, and the rainfall in previous days. Angry or serene, the many falls offer plenty of excuses for pauses.

Eventually, the path starts making a distinct climb to the left, away from the water. But just as you feel you're finally leaving the river behind, you reach a white-blazed spur trail breaking off to the right. Take this trail. If you remained on the yellow trail, you would go through the edge of the old picnic area, now all but forgotten, to hook up with the Firetower Trail. The yellow trail no longer goes to Stepstone Falls itself.

To see the falls, take the white cutoff back toward the stream. The terrain is very rocky here, but in less than ½ mile you reach the most impressive falls yet. These are natural; there was no need to "improve" upon what already existed. The river sweeps over the wide, flat rocks as if gliding from shelf to shelf, or step to step — hence the name Stepstone Falls.

Another wooden bridge, this one more elaborate than those you used earlier, enables you to cross the stream just below the finest set of falls. The white-marked trail also crosses the bridge, goes left a few hundred feet to an old auto bridge, and returns on the opposite side of the stream, so you can easily walk all the way around Stepstone. After you complete the circle, you can take an unmarked path from the footbridge uphill, via stone steps, to the old picnic grounds. You can walk through it, pick up the yellow trail once more behind a shelter house at the far end, turn left, and retrace your walk to your car.

18. Mount Tom Trail

A roundabout route to Mt. Tom, past the ruins of a gristmill, over rocky cliffs, and through a reforestation project

Hiking distance: 6½ miles
Hiking time: 3½ hours

THIS WANDERING, ROUNDABOUT ROUTE UP TO Mount Tom in Exeter features a wide variety of attractions. Along the way, you cross rushing brooks and pause atop rocky cliffs; you inspect the remains of an old gristmill and stroll through a thriving reforestation project.

As a bonus, you can shorten your walk without retracing your steps by turning and walking a roadway back to your car. Walk this entire 6½-mile route, however, and you will avoid the paved road except for the few steps it takes to twice cross the highway and a few more to use a bridge. You will be returning along a quiet, seldom-used dirt road.

ACCESS

Mount Tom Trail, another of the many Appalachian Mountain Club paths in the Arcadia Management Area, begins along RI 165 at a spot known as Appie Crossing, about 2½ miles west of RI 3. This is the end of the Arcadia Trail (see Walk 20) and virtually across the highway from the beginning of the John B. Hudson Trail (Walk 19). There is little parking space at Appie Crossing, however, and returning there would mean a walk along the heavily used RI 165 or retracing your route, so I recommend driving a few hundred yards farther west and parking near the West Exeter Baptist Church at the corner of Frosty Hollow Road. Look for a barred lane coming

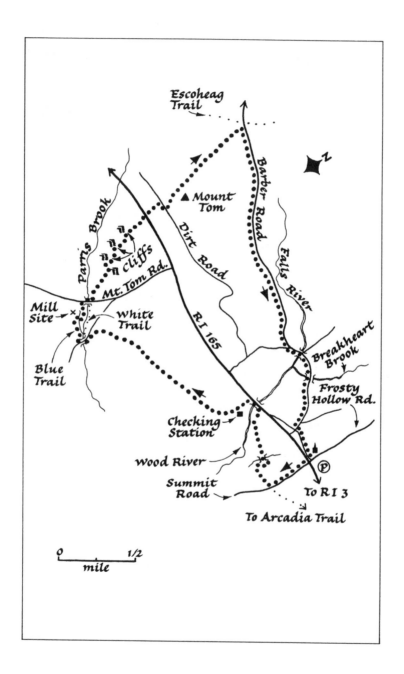

Escoheag
Trail

Barber
Road

N

Mount
Tom

Dirt
Road

Falls
River

Parris Brook

Cliffs

Mt. Tom Rd.

RI 165

Mill
Site

White
Trail

Blue
Trail

Breakheart
Brook

Frosty
Hollow Rd.

Checking
Station

Wood River

Summit
Road

Ⓟ

To RI 3

To Arcadia Trail

0   1/2
    mile

out of the forest near the front of the church; this will be your return route. Please do not park in the church lot itself, particularly if you arrive on a Sunday morning.

TRAIL

To start your walk, cross RI 165 and go 0.2 mile down a gravel road called Summit Road, directly opposite Frosty Hollow Road. The white-blazed hiking trail crosses Summit Road, so when you reach the trail, turn right and you are on your way. (You could just as easily start by walking the dirt road in front of the church, but given a choice, I prefer using roads at the end of my walks, when I start feeling weary.)

You go downhill at first, climb a hill, then swing around to a brook, which you will cross on a bridge made of a pile of small logs. In a few more minutes, you will reach Wood River, a popular trout stream. Lanes run along both shores for the fishermen. It would be shorter to wade through the stream and pick up the trail on the other side, but the blazes lead you to the right over the RI 165 bridge and back left on a gravel lane, past a Quonset hut that is used as a checking station in hunting season.

Now, you are entering the state's Wood River Valley Reforestation Project, an area replanted after 7,500 acres of timberland were destroyed in 1951 in one of the worst forest fires in Rhode Island history. Thousands of 30-foot pines thrive here, and all the scars from that tragic fire have vanished.

The trail follows the access roads, so it is wide, level, and sandy. Walking this area in springtime is totally delightful. In May, during warbler migration, the pines are alive with the pert little birds. Young rabbits lope down the lanes, more inquisitive than afraid, and often you will find deer tracks in the soft sand. Violets bloom beside the roads, adding color and beauty to your walk.

In fall and early winter, you are likely to meet hunters here, seeking the deer, rabbits, pheasants, quail, and grouse, but in other seasons you may have this area to yourself.

Watch the blazes carefully; there are several side roads. The trail leaves the pine grove when you reach a gravel road. Follow the road left a short distance to a stream. The white-blazed trail turns right just before the bridge and follows the stream, but it is better to cross the bridge and follow a blue-marked alternate path on the opposite shore. The blue trail is not as open, but it allows you to visit the old mill site.

The stream is called Parris Brook, and the blue trail soon swings left to follow a separate channel. This is a millrace that leads back to the stone foundation of a gristmill built before 1800 and abandoned now far longer than it was used. Water diverted from the stream continues to run through the mill's immense stoneworks, but the wheel it turned has long since vanished. Still, it is one of the more impressive of the many abandoned mill sites along Rhode Island trails. It invites inspection.

The trail quickly rejoins Parris Brook, which rumbles constantly as it cascades down man-made trout falls. The trail then leads you out to a paved road, Mount Tom Road. Turn right, cross a bridge, and then bear left into the woods.

Now you are starting the climb toward the cliffs. Although relatively steep, this section of trail is not difficult because it follows an overgrown woods lane. Young oaks are reclaiming the lane but stone embankments and walls still reveal its original profile.

Within minutes, you are straddling a ridge. Cutoff paths on both sides lead to rock ledges. The higher you climb, the more ledges you find, and the better the views. Atop one overlook, facing east, you can see for miles, and the scenery is all trees. You may find it hard to believe this is tame, densely populated Rhode Island; it looks for all the world like Vermont or New Hampshire.

Other outcroppings farther on face south and west and they also look over forested valleys. Pines and oaks dominate, but in spring an occasional dogwood in flower adds a dash of color.

The trail along the ridge is all rock. The adventurous and nimble can take shortcuts up and over the boulders. The less agile should follow the trail around the huge rocks. Both routes wind up at the same places — at the edge of ledges that drop straight off. It would be a long fall, so watch your step. At the bottom of the cliffs rest great slabs of stone chopped off by the glaciers. They remind me of immense slices of gray cheese whacked off some giant wedge.

More up and down scrambling is ahead but fewer cliffs, and shortly, you descend to RI 165 once more. You have now walked almost 3½ miles, and you can return to your car by simply turning right and following the highway to your car.

But Mount Tom itself still looms ahead. The trail crosses the highway and immediately starts upward. Here there are fewer rocks,

76

no cliffs, and no open vistas. For the most part, it is an easy but uneventful hike up and over the crest, which at 460 feet is one of the highest spots in the area.

Unlike most hills, it is difficult to tell when you are at the summit. After the initial climb, the trail runs straight and relatively level for its last mile. Bushes and saplings crowd in on both sides, and in places it is deeply rutted from trail bike use.

The trail ends on the dirt lane once called Barber Road. Just to the left, the Escoheag Trail (Walk 14) crosses the road. To return to your car, however, turn right and follow the old road. Closed to cars and trunks except during hunting and fishing seasons, the road runs downhill about 2 miles, passing plenty of forest scenes and game management fields and crossing two streams that merge shortly below here to form the Wood River. In spring, this is a delightful walk with a great deal of bird activity.

Shortly after crossing the second bridge, you'll reach a wide, open area. Snowmobilers park their trucks here in winter and dog sled races are also held. Look for a barred lane on the far left; it leads to the church and your car. If unsure which lane to take, however, you can follow the main road out to RI 165. Your car is 0.3 mile to the left.

19. John B. Hudson Trail

A panoramic view, a stroll through pine groves, a view of a fish ladder, a wealth of songbirds — a good introductory hike for children

Hiking distance: 3 miles
Hiking time: 1½-2 hours

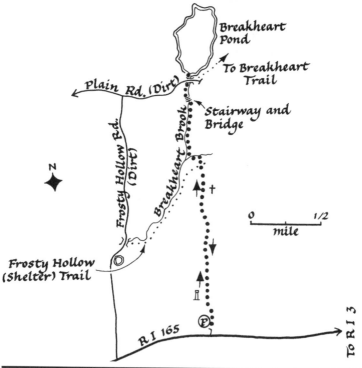

THE JOHN B. HUDSON TRAIL, NAMED FOR ONE

of Rhode Island's hiking pioneers, is one of the oldest in the state trail system and one of the shortest, yet it remains one of the most popular. It should be; it's a gem.

It is less than 1½ miles long, running from RI 165 to Breakheart Pond in the Arcadia Management Area in Exeter, but sections of it are downright dazzling, particularly in late spring, when the thickets of mountain laurel are in bloom, and in the winter, when the gurgling stream that it crosses is as pretty as any picture with ice and snow.

The trail also offers a panoramic view from an observation tower, a stroll through surging pine groves and past a tiny cemetery, and, at its end, a look at a concrete fish ladder and a picturesque pond. All in all, it packs a lot of highlights into 1½ miles or 3 miles, round-trip.

Part of the region's vast "Yellow-Dot Trail" system, the Hudson begins almost directly across RI 165 from the end of the Arcadia Trail (see Walk 20). At Breakheart Pond, it links with Breakheart Trail (Walk 16). Along the way, it also crosses the newer, white-blazed Frosty Hollow Trail (Walk 15).

This is a good trail for giving small children a taste of hiking. The first section, which includes the tower, is flat and easy walking. Later, there is some scrambling up and down where the trail swings down to a stream. That area is particularly muddy and treacherous in early spring, so it might be wise to hold off until at least May. The laurel usually blooms in late May or early June.

ACCESS

To reach the start, take RI 165 2.6 miles west from RI 3. Check your odometer because the point, although marked by a small sign on a tree, is easily missed. A narrow, angling lane takes you to a parking area, on the right, that is veiled from the road by trees.

TRAIL

Young pines are beginning to crowd the trail, and often there are numerous songbirds along this early stretch — warblers, catbirds, and thrushes in spring and summer, chickadees and white-throated sparrows in fall and winter.

In just a matter of minutes, at the first opening in the pines, look for a white-marked side trail to the left. It leads to the wooden tower, which is obscured by leaves in summer. It is a climb of only 25 steps, but from the top you can see miles to the west, and the view is one of surprising wildness. Even in winter, you cannot see a single house or road. Only wooded hills.

Back on the trail, you begin reaching the laurel thickets that seem to be larger and more magnificent each year. You will be in and out of laurel throughtout this walk, and when your timing is right, this can be a stroll through virtual tunnels of flowers.

The little family cemetery, guarded by stone walls, is just to the right of the trail in a grove of tall pines. The few legible dates range from the 1830s to the 1850s. There, among the pines, it is truly a peaceful final resting place.

Soon after you cross a woods road you'll see the white-blazed path called the Shelter Trail (I prefer calling it the Frosty Hollow Trail) and then the Hudson begins its descent toward a stream called Breakheart Brook. At one point, you follow a brook down a steep, laurel-covered slope, and hop back and forth across the brook numerous times before reaching the stream.

Then, for a considerable distance, you follow the shoreline. Once this area caused great problems for walkers because of mud, but now there are step stones in many places, some small bridges, and many wooden runoff channels on the slopes. You are still likely to get muddy feet here, particularly in spring, but it is worth the risk. The river, splashing and tumbling over thousands of rocks, is spectacular when framed by the overhanging laurel or fringed with ice or snow.

The trail climbs onto higher ground (from where you can hear the stream even when it is out of sight) until you reach a wooden stairway down a particularly steep slope. Built in 1980 by a youth group, the steps lead to a bridge over the stream. The trail then runs through a small picnic area along the opposite shore and out to the gravel road beside Breakheart Pond. For a description of the fish ladder dam and the pond, see Walk 16.

If you are ambitious, you can walk an open lane all the way around the pond, about 1½ miles, or you can simply linger awhile and enjoy the spot. The walk back to your car may be just a bit tougher than the walk in, since you will be going uphill more than down, but it will be just as pretty.

20. Arcadia Trail

A car-shuttle walk to see majestic beech trees, gurgling brooks, and a lovely pond

Hiking distance: 4 miles
Hiking time: 2 hours

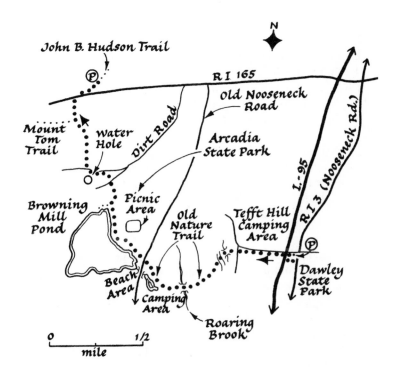

ONCE, ARCADIA TRAIL IN EXETER WAS AMONG

the most heavily used hiking paths in Rhode Island. Now, only segments of it see much use, but most of the features that were among its highlights years ago still exist.

This trail, one of many connecting yellow-blazed paths developed by the Appalachian Mountain Club in the vast forests of Exeter and West Greenwich, runs through impressive stands of beech trees, crosses rock-ribbed brooks, skirts the edge of lily-pad ponds, cuts through a campground and a popular state park, and then wanders through a dense woods punctuated with boulders and stone walls.

You will also find bridges constructed by the Youth Conservation Corps in the late 1970s, an unusual "water hole" built by a Civilian Conservation Corps crew in the 1930s, and what is left of a nature trail designed to identify trees and plants for hikers.

ACCESS

Begin your walk at Dawley State Park on RI 3 (Nooseneck Road) just south of RI 165 in Exeter. For a one-way trip, leave a car at the John B. Hudson Trail (see Walk 19) on RI 165, 2.5 miles west of the RI 3 junction. (Arcadia Trail also links with the Mount Tom Trail (Walk 18) just before emerging on RI 165, almost directly across the highway from the start of the Hudson Trail.) Just up the Hudson lane, not 50 yards from the highway but hidden in the trees, is a parking area for several cars. A walk to the start of the Mount Tom Trail is just over 3½ miles; continuing to a car in the Hudson Trail lot makes a hike of close to 4 miles.

TRAIL

Back at Dawley State Park, pick up the yellow blazes just behind the log shelter building. Dawley once was a popular picnic area but is virtually unused now except by walkers. The trail runs through surging undergrowth but reaches a gravel road in a few minutes. Turn left on the road and follow it under two bridges built for I-95.

The gravel road is Tefft Hill Road, and it quickly runs to Tefft Hill Camping Area, a tenting complex. The trail cuts through the campground, then, at a junction of gravel roads, plunges into the forest. You will be dropping down a rock-strewn slope and quickly leaving all the campground activity behind.

Arcadia Trail runs along the shore of picturesque Browning Mill Pond.

In minutes, you cross on brook on a bridge, then step over two others on rocks. Magnificent beeches — tall, straight, and majestic with their smooth, gray bark and spreading branches — compete with the stony path and the gurgling brooks for your attention. This section is particularly inviting in autumn, when the beech leaves turn a golden brown and squirrels scamper about while collecting the little beechnuts.

There may be more beech trees on this walk than anywhere else in the state, but unfortunately you also are apt to find more carvings on the trees — names, initials, dates, hearts, etc. Most of the markings are quite old; apparently the practice is not as popular now.

When you reach a stretch of trail that is relatively level and rock-free, you are nearing what was a nature trail developed by the Youth Conservation Corps. Most of the identification signs for the lower plants have now vanished, but you can still see a few nailed to larger trees.

After crossing a log bridge over a hurrying stream called Roaring Brook and then a wooden walkway over a wet, rocky area, you can begin looking to the left for a small, shallow pond decorated in summer with water lilies. The trail stays several yards from the pond but cutoffs run left to the water's edge.

The trail swerves away from the pond, then returns. Near the end of the pond you will see a fork going left over the bridge, where water spills into a stream. This path offers good views of the pond, but the yellow-blazed trail takes the right fork, curving through the woods and out to a paved road called Old Nooseneck Road.

You are now in Arcadia State Park. The trail runs directly across the road and into a picnic area on the shore of Browning Mill Pond, known locally as Arcadia Pond. A beach area lies to the left along the roadway, and there is a campground just down the road, also to your left.

At a pavilion, the trail swings down to the pond's edge and then follows the shoreline. This pond attracts many fishermen as well as picnickers and swimmers. It is delightful in fall, when the trees across the water are ablaze in color. There are more likely pads here and often swallows and other birds swoop over the water in pursuit of insects.

When you reach the end of the pond, watch for a fork. The worn path continues following the shore, but the yellow blazes turn right, up a rocky slope. There are many pines here, and in May and June, hundreds of pink ladyslipper flowers.

The trail crosses a narrow woods road, goes up and over a stony ridge, then emerges on a dirt road now all but abandoned. Turn left on the road. After rounding a bend, where dogwoods dress the woods edge in white each spring, you will see the "water hole" on the left. Stone walls and a wooden railing enclose the miniature, square reservoir built to hold water from a tiny brook that passes beneath the road. Similar basins are scattered through the area but few are along public hiking routes.

A few yards farther, the trail returns to the woods on the right. For the next ¾ mile, you amble around the side of a hill through a most pleasant woods. The path is narrow and shady; undergrowth is dense in places.

Finally, you mount a ridge that features angular boulders, and then it is downhill the rest of the way. You pass a white-blazed cutoff on the left that is the start of the Mount Tom Trail, and drop through a soft, boggy section. When you reach RI 165, turn right and cross to the lane marked with an arrow for the John B. Hudson Trail. It is only a few more steps to your car.

21. Wickaboxet Trail

A prime wildlife walk and a climactic vista of the state's forgotten area.

Hiking distance: 5 miles
Hiking time: 2½ hours

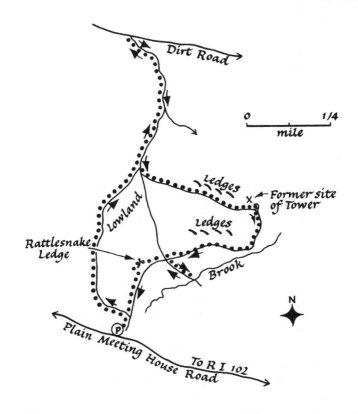

ONLY THE MOST KNOWLEDGEABLE OF RHODE
Island outdoorsmen know Wickaboxet Management Area. It lies in
a remote part of the state, and has been virtually forgotten. Yet, it
can be a marvelous place to walk.

Wickaboxet, the smallest of the state management areas (405
acres), is in West Greenwich, just south of the Coventry line. It
was the first state forest and once was extensively used for picnics
and other outdoor recreation, but in recent years it has been over-
shadowed by the much larger Arcadia Management Area a few
miles south.

These days, only a few hunters use the place in autumn and
occasionally horsemen ride along the old roads. Young people sometimes climb the area's featured attraction, Rattlesnake Ledge, but
for the most part, Wickaboxet has been left to the grouse, squirrels,
deer and songbirds.

There are no marked hiking trails in Wickaboxet. Instead, you
follow the woods roads. The 5-mile route described here runs the
entire length of the state property, then returns to the interior for
a stroll past rock ledges, and finally finishes with a climactic climb
up Rattlesnake Ledge, which offers one of the finest vistas anywhere
in the state.

ACCESS

At this writing, there is not even a sign identifying Wickaboxet.
To find the only entrance, drive RI 102 to Plain Meeting House
Road, then go west for 3 miles to a small parking lot off the right
side of the road.

TRAIL

The entrance road forks almost immediately. Unless you are interested only in Rattlesnake Ledge, walk to the left. This is an easy,
grassy lane that runs slightly uphill as it curls to the right. The
woods here are rather open and you will notice the roadway is cut
several inches below the forest floor. In this section you might see
faded white blazes on a few trees; disregard them, they no longer
serve as a guide.

Birds abound in Wickaboxet. Flycatchers, woodpeckers,

thrushes, warblers, and other woodland birds are constant companions. As you progress through areas where the trees are smaller and bushes more abundant, you will find far more birds — waxwings, thrashers, grosbeaks, towhees, and so many more. There will be squirrels and chipmunks along the trail, too, and occasionally you may come upon a grouse dusting itself on the lane. Wildlife is one of the prime attractions of Wickaboxet.

Before you have gone a mile, your road will merge with another lane coming in from the right. Continue walking north. The lane winds back and forth a bit over low, sandy ridges. Throughout this area, the trees are small. When you reach a spot where a larger tree has been felled across the lane, you are nearing the end of state property. Just beyond, the lane runs onto a grassy road, called Welsh Hollow Road on old maps, that serves as the northern boundary. Welsh Hollow is an inviting road, but land in both directions is private property, so return down the sandy lane you just walked.

As you return, you pass a narrow cutoff lane, now on your left. If you want a good indication of what happens when such lanes are abandoned, take this cutoff a hundred yards or so. The lane is choked by young pines, some ten or fifteen feet tall, in a section dominated by hardwoods.

Back on the main roadway, retrace your steps to the Y intersection, turn left, then left again almost immediately at another junction. You will now be on a lane that runs along some low rock ledges, with taller trees on each side. At the end of the rocky ridge, a side trail curls around left and deadends atop the ridge. Here, you may find some concrete anchors left from a vanished firetower.

The road downhill makes sweeping turns to the right twice, running below another section of ridges. When you reach a crossroads, take a look at the lane to the left. It is grassy and shady — most inviting. I walked it once, intending only to check out a small brook that crosses the road, and was rewarded with a sighting of a large deer that leaped up and bounded through the forest, flashing its white flag of a tail at me.

Just beyond this crossroads, along the main road, look to the right. Not far off the lane looms a massive rock outcropping, Rattlesnake Ledge. It is doubtful any rattlesnakes remain, but be careful anyway in climbing to the top of this ledge. A fall can be potentially more painful than a snakebite.

The view from the top is delightful, and surprising after walking more than 4 miles over relatively level terrain. You can see for miles over the treetops; in fact, your view is of virtually unbroken forest, quite likely the longest such vista still available in Rhode Island.

Back from the cliff, a well-worn path winds back down to the roadway. From here, it is only about 0.3 mile back to your car.

22. Trestle Trail

A car-shuttle walk along an abandoned railroad bed to observe wildlife and a beaver dam

Hiking distance: 7 miles
Hiking time: 3-3½ hours

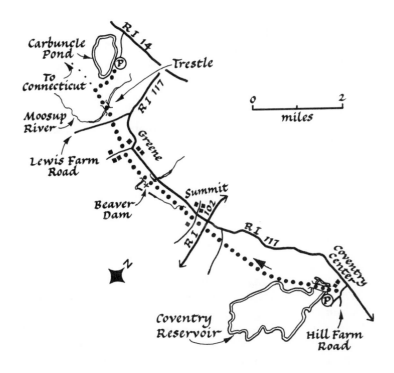

LONG AND STRAIGHT, AND STILL A BIT DIFFER-
ent. That's the Trestle Trail in Coventry, a path that has changed
in recent years but now is interesting for new reasons.

When *25 Walks in Rhode Island* was published in 1978, Trestle
Trail was one of the newest walking routes in the state, a 7-mile
path that followed an abandoned railroad bed from Coventry Center
to the Connecticut line. Since then, motorcyclists have used the
trail far more than walkers and the path itself has deteriorated in
places, but there have been compensating improvements. The surroundings are far more wild now, with the continued growth of the
bordering trees and bushes, and wildlife has increased accordingly.
In addition to a great deal of bird activity, you will see squirrels
and deer tracks, and if you are lucky, a beaver or two. One of the
highlights of the walk is a beaver dam recently built beneath one
of the old railroad bridges.

Each year, vestiges of the old New York, New Haven, and
Hartford railroad are less visible, but there are still many rotting
ties lying along the embankments and one section still features
telegraph poles that long ago were swallowed by the surging forest.
The stone embankments themselves and the bridges, many now
hidden by vines and bushes, tell part of the path's history, and
occasionally, the sharp-eyed can still find a railroad spike along the
trail. For the most part, however, the trail more and more resembles
a woods road.

Because the footing is solid and the path still several feet wide,
the Trestle Trail is one you can walk almost immediately after a
rain, or on a dewy summer morning, when other woods paths would
get you drenched. It's a great substitute.

ACCESS

This is a one-way walk, so it is best to leave a car at Carbuncle
Pond, a popular fishing spot just east of the Connecticut line on
RI 14. Drive along the dirt entrance road as far as you can; you'll
be finishing your walk at this spot.

To reach the trail's start from Carbuncle, drive RI 14 east to RI
117, then follow 117 as it goes south and then east. In Coventry
Center, take Hill Farm Road to the right a very short distance to
a small parking area on the right, beside a pond. The path begins

behind large concrete blocks that bar cars and trucks from driving the lane.

TRAIL

On the left is Coventry Reservoir, often called Stump Pond, and on the right is a smaller pond. You quickly cross a bridge over water that links the ponds. Two of the biggest changes in the trail are immediately evident. No longer is the path level; now it undulates considerably in places, perhaps a result of its heavy use by cycles and three-wheeled all-terrain vehicles. The many low bushes and flowers that characterized this stretch previously have been crowded out by taller trees, which in many places now meet overhead, creating long, green tunnels for the walkers.

Bird activity has grown along with the trees. Expect to see and/or hear thrushes, catbirds, tanagers, flycatchers, blue jays, orioles, woodpeckers, and warblers as you walk the lane. On one summer walk here, I came across a family of crested flycatchers, a family of orioles, and was treated to the sight of a brilliant scarlet tanager male and its olive, nearly yellow, mate drinking from a water puddle almost at my feet.

There are numerous side trails made by cyclists but ignore them all; your route runs straight ahead. Because the railroad was built as level as possible, you will be alternately walking higher than the surrounding woodland and lower than it. When you pass lowlands, note the wealth of ferns carpeting the forest floor. When your route cuts through ridges, notice the boulders and remnants of stone walls in the woods.

In the first 2 miles, you cross three bridges, but they are becoming easy to miss because of the surging undergrowth. Most are built of large stone blocks cemented together. You also will pass a point where a paved road and a new housing development run up to the trail on the left. A gravel road crosses the trail and disappears into the woods on the right.

Shortly, you find yourself well above the surrounding forest, higher than the tops of the telegraph poles still standing in the woods on the right. Trees now dwarf the poles, stretching at least twice as high. You cross a paved road at about 2.7 miles, then pass through a section where the trail slices through rock ledges, leaving

A beaver dam beneath one of the old railroad bridges adds a pleasing touch to the Trestle Trail.

green, mossy walls on both sides. Now you are nearing RI 102 and the village of Summit. The bridge for 102 is high overhead — so high you might not notice it — but you will notice, beneath the bridge, the long, seemingly-permanent water hole that resembles a muddy pond. To pass the water hazard, stay to the right where an alternate path is being created on the shoulder.

The next crossing — you see a horse farm on the left and houses on the right — is a paved road in the village of Summit, most of which lies to your right. This is approximately 3½ miles from your start and represents the halfway point in your walk.

Beyond the village, there are areas of water on both sides of the trail, particularly the left, a result of the arrival of beavers. They have dammed up several brooks in Coventry in recent years and flooded a number of low-lying areas. They are most active at night so your chances of seeing beavers are slim, but quiet observation as you walk through here may pay off. The new marshes also attract other wildlife — herons, ducks, bullfrogs — that can be more easily seen.

The stretch between Summit and the next village, Greene, is delightful. Not only is there the chance of seeing beavers, but also you pass through groves of vibrant pines and open areas where wild roses, blueberries, blackberries, and wildflowers are thriving. The only drawback in this area is some water holes that may force you to detour through the brush.

When you reach a metal bridge set on huge stone blocks you are nearing Greene. Pause a moment on the bridge and look down, to the left. Almost below the bridge is a beaver dam that not only has created a sizable pond, but also has made a noisy waterfall beneath the trail. It's a good place to rest.

At Greene, beside silver train wheels mounted on a concrete base, is a plaque that describes the history of the railroad as well as that of the village.

The next segment of the walk, between Greene and a gravel road called Lewis Farm Road, is the most difficult. Larger stones were spread over this section when Trestle Trail was established and they are hard on the feet. Fortunately, you cross the area quickly.

Once past Lewis Farm Road, you can see the trestle for which the trail was named. Hung about fifty feet above the Mossup River, this bridge, now equipped with chain-link fences on both sides, offers splendid views of the lovely trout stream as well as the surrounding countryside. It is one more place to linger.

Less than ¼ mile beyond the trestle, just as the trail makes a slight curve left, take a well-worn cutoff trail that runs downhill to the right. This will take you to Carbuncle Pond and your car.

23. Parker Woodland-Coventry

An historic walk to old farms and mills, and cairns deep in the woods

Hiking distance: 3 miles
Hiking time: 2-2½ hours

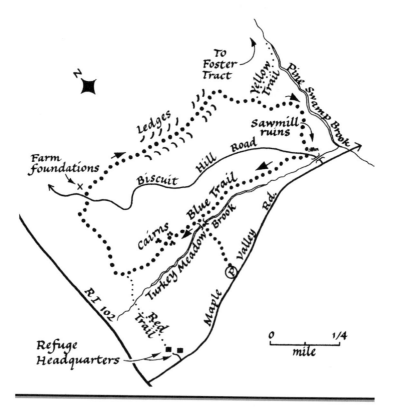

A WALK THROUGH PARKER WOODLAND IS A

stroll through history. It enables you to take a look at the Rhode Island of 200 years ago in the stone remains of mills and farmhouses and other buildings, as well as taking a look at mysterious stone cairns.

This trail is the Coventry Tract of Parker Woodland, a large and increasingly popular area owned by the Audubon Society of Rhode Island. The refuge also spills over into Foster (see Walk 24).

Parker Woodland lies along Maple Valley Road in an area where farms were abandoned long ago and the land has been reclaimed by forest. Once, the area was a lively — and deadly — place. Two taverns along the old road were known for the ruffians they attracted, and tales of shootings punctuate the region's history and lore. Some local residents still speak of troubled spirits roaming the older houses.

Now, however, Parker Woodland is quiet, almost eerie, with many reminders of the past silently reposing beside and beneath vigorous saplings and bushes.

ACCESS

To reach the Coventry Tract, turn east from RI 102 onto Maple Valley Road. The first house on the left is the refuge's headquarters. Stop in for a pamphlet that describes areas marked by numbered posts along the trail. The parking lot for hikers is nearly ¼ mile farther down Maple Valley Road, also on the left. There, you will find a large trail map etched into a wooden sign.

TRAIL

Immediately, you come face to face with history. At the trail's start you'll see a sign describing what a team of archaeologists from Brown University found, in 1983, when they explored a home site on the spot. They also studied two charcoal processing sites farther down the trail and a large farm that once prospered far back in the woods. Signs at those sites also provide insight into life in the area in the 18th century.

The archaeologists, however, did not attempt to solve the mystery of the stone cairns, and perhaps it's better this way. Now each walker can speculate on just who built the pyramid-shaped monuments, and why. Were they built by Indians for burial or religious rituals? Or by pre-Columbian explorers who were marking their way by the stars? Or simply by some fussy farmer who wasn't satisfied with just throwing the rocks onto a pile?

You pass the charcoal pits quickly and then cross Turkey Meadow Brook before reaching the main, blue-blazed trail. Go left and in just a few minutes you reach the cairns — dozens of them — scattered through the woods. Take time to look them over and note their workmanship, while theorizing on their origins. Many are filled with stones so meticulously fitted together they are still solid after more than two centuries. Restrict your study to looking, however; Audubon allows no disturbing of the cairns.

The trail remains rocky as it loops through magnificent groves of beech trees. At one point, you pass a red-marked side trail (which runs to the Parker headquarters on Maple Valley Road), then the blue trail begins swinging to the right. The walking is easier here for some distance, until you reach the old farm.

First, you find the foundation of a barn. Then, on the opposite side of a dirt road lined on both sides by stone walls, you'll see the

The mysterious stone cairns scattered through Parker Woodland have never been explained.

cellar hole for the house, remains of a small out-building, and the family's stone-lined well. A sign provides substantial background on the farm, including dates and names.

The dirt road you cross (Biscuit Hill Road) is a shortcut back to Turkey Meadow Brook and many walkers use it, possibly as much for its own history as for the steps it saves. Biscuit Hill Road supposedly received its names when a wagon load of biscuits meant for Rochambeau's army was spilled here during the Revolutionary War. If you take the road to the right, you will reach the brook at an old sawmill.

The main trail, however, returns to the woods through the "backyard" of the farmhouse, and circles through an extremely rocky area. You will pass ledges and boulders of various sizes and shapes, gradually working your way downhill.

At an immense boulder, a yellow-marked trail breaks off to the left. This is the connector path to the Foster Tract of Parker Woodland and it is worth walking because it runs through a beautiful rocky area beside a brook. This is Pine Swamp Brook and you will be walking upstream, advancing along a series of falls and pools. For a description of the forest beyond the brook, see Walk 24.

When you return to the blue trail, go left. You will climb through woods to the end of Biscuit Hill Road, this time emerging near the impressive stone remains of the sawmill, just to your left. Most of the dam still stands, although the center has been removed. Extensive flat-faced stone work shows the flume and sluiceway that carried the water under the road, where it dropped into a deep cellarlike excavation — again lined with flat stones — that held the huge waterwheel.

Originally, this was a vertical sawmill, but around 1908, after most of the virgin timber of the area had been harvested, it was altered for a steam-powered saw. A mess hall, bunkhouse, and horse barn were added, and their foundations also remain.

From here, return to the blue trail and follow it left along Turkey Meadow Brook. In less than ¼ mile, you are back at the bridge just downhill from the parking lot.

24. Parker Woodland-Foster

A forest walk through former farmland and beside stone quarries

Hiking distance: 4½ miles
Hiking time: 2½-3 hours

Yellow Connector Trail

Farm Site

To Pierce Rd.

N

Stone Quarry

Blue Trail

Pig Hill Rd.

Blue

Pine Swamp Bk.

Biscuit Hill Road

Trail

Stone Quarry

sawmill ruins

Maple Valley Road

0   1/2
mile

To R I 102

THE FOSTER TRACT OF PARKER WOODLAND IS

not nearly as well known — and therefore walked far less often — as its neighbor the Coventry Tract (see Walk 23) but is a gem in its own right.

Basically, it is a forest walk that loops through what was once farmland. You pass numerous stone walls, several cellar holes and foundations of vanished buildings and two small stone quarries. On the 3-hour, 4½-mile route described here, you will also visit a picturesque brook that tumbles down a rocky ravine.

ACCESS

The Foster Tract has its own starting point and a small parking lot, but access can be difficult, with long drives on gravel and dirt roads, so I recommend starting and ending at the parking lot for the Coventry Tract. This way, you'll hit some of the historical highlights of that walk as well as use the short connector trail between the two tracts. The connector is among the prettiest areas of the entire Parker Woodland.

If you want to walk only the 2.3-mile Foster trail, you can enter from Old Plainfield Pike, about a mile east of RI 102. Take gravel Pierce Road south until its end, then go right and continue as the gravel turns to dirt. Old maps show this as Pig Hill Road. The parking area is another mile into the forest.

TRAIL

For those who start at the Coventry parking lot off Maple Valley Road, take a few minutes to look over the signs at the archaeological digs at an old homesite and, farther along the trail, a charcoal processing site. Then cross Turkey Meadow Brook and take the blue-blazed trail to the right. (A yellow-blazed trail runs more directly to the Foster tract, but it is less interesting and not as well-defined). The blue trail follows the brook until crossing a woods road (Biscuit Hill Road) and passing the remains of a sawmill a few yards to the right (both the road and the mill are described in Walk 23). The trail goes into a rocky area, swings near a tiny stream called Pine Swamp Brook, and goes back uphill briefly until reaching the connector trail, with a sign "To Foster Tract," just beyond an immense boulder.

Go right to the connector (the yellow blazes are not easy to see in autumn, when much of the underbrush is yellow and golden-brown). The path returns to Pine Swamp Brook, which tumbles down a ravine filled with jumbled boulders. It's an appealing area, particularly where the path drops down to the water's edge, enabling you to advance upstream. The brook is a series of falls and pools. When you see a low rock dam that creates a larger pool, it's time to cross the brook. There is a log for a bridge, but in most seasons the brook is so narrow you can step over on the boulders.

Still on the yellow trail, you soon leave the brook, climb uphill, and in a matter of minutes reach the intersection with the Foster Tract trail, marked in blue. Turn right here, and you will quickly arrive at the parking lot along Pig Hill Road.

Cross the road, go through a brushy area where the trail is narrow, and soon you will be heading downhill. On the left is a rugged ledge with several small caves at its foot, then you walk through open, pleasant woods as you circle a small swamp.

Off the trail, to the right, is a section of broken and piled stones, left over from quarry operations, and when the leaves are down you'll be able to see the foundation of a building that is worth inspecting. From here, the trail curves left and you will pass trees with signs that mark the boundary of the Parker refuge.

The walking alternates from descents through rocky lowlands to hilly but easy woodlands for some distance. You will pass a three-sided stone foundation and skirt the edge of a second quarry before crossing Pig Hill Road for the second time.

After passing through a grove of tall pines, one of the few areas in this second-growth forest where you find mature trees, you reach the "fields" of a vanished farm. Boundaries are still marked by stone walls, some high and straight, others little more than tumbledown piles. You pass one small cellar hole, probably a barn or outbuilding, then swing through a break in a wall, curl around to the left and reach a virtual network of walls.

Across the wall on your left is the cellar hole of the farmhouse. Taking up half of its cellar space is the huge foundation for the chimney. On the far side are the steps and there is a tree growing exactly where the long-ago farmers climbed in and out of the cellar. Out a few yards from the stairway, hidden beneath a huge flat stone, is the family's well. Its circular, stone-lined walls are a work of art and invite inspection, but be very careful. Old wells can be dangerous.

From the farm site, the trail drops down a steep hill, curves left and runs near Pine Swamp Brook again. Just before you reach the brook, you'll pass, on your left, a stone fireplace built against a boulder. The rocks, green with lichens, hint of being there for ages. Was it part of a cabin, or merely a project of somebody camping for the night? Nobody knows.

When you climb out of the brook's valley, you'll be back in second-growth woods — mostly oaks — and will pass numerous stone walls that seem bewildering. They wander at all angles and few are connected; just lines of rocks for some distance, then they end. Probably simply a means of clearing some of the fields of rocks.

At the fork with the yellow connector trail, turn right and return to your car in the Coventry lot. When you reach the bridge at the mill site at the bottom of Biscuit Hill Road, you can go out onto Maple Valley Road and finish your walk on the paved roadway.

25. Gainer Dam

An excellent walk for birders and a view of the Gainer Dam and Scituate Reservoir

Hiking distance: 2.8 miles
Hiking time: 1½ hours

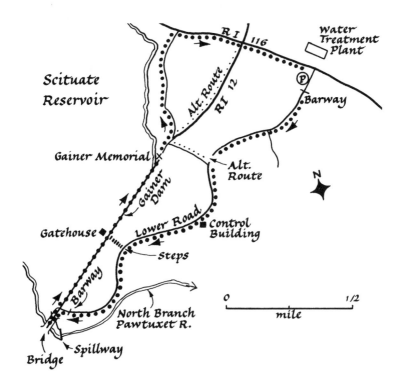

THIS WALK IS DIFFERENT. UNLIKE MOST OF THE hikes in this book, this one is on pavement all the way, and you are strictly forbidden from wandering off into the surrounding woodlands. Still, it is a charming stroll that can be as short as slightly more than 1 mile or stretched out to almost 3 miles.

One of the few walks in the central part of Rhode Island, this route takes you across the massive Gainer Memorial Dam that created the vast Scituate Reservoir and loops through a quiet area of forest and grass on a road closed to vehicular traffic.

In most seasons, it is an excellent walk for birders, offering glimpses of field birds (robins, meadowlarks, killdeer), woods birds (chickadees, nuthatches, thrushes), and lake birds (mergansers, ducks, geese). It is particularly inviting in early spring, when many migrating waterfowl stop over on the reservoir, a time when many other trails are too muddy for pleasant walking.

Because reservoir land is off-limits to everyone, wildlife is thriving. Without leaving the roads, I've seen otters, raccoons, and numerous chipmunks and squirrels, plus wild turkeys and grouse, in addition to waterfowl and songbirds.

ACCESS

The walk's start is located on RI 116 just south of RI 12 in Scituate. Look for a barred road directly across from a large water treatment plant. There is ample parking space on the road before the barway. If you arrive on a weekend morning, you are likely to find several cars here as this has become an increasingly popular place for joggers and walkers.

TRAIL

To the right, as you pass the barway, is one of the open, lawn-like fields of grass you will see on this walk. On one recent spring morning, I counted 24 robins strutting about within 50 feet of my path. On the left is a stand of pine trees in precise rows, obviously planted as part of the reservoir project.

On both sides of the roadway you will see yellow signs that warn: "NO TRESPASSING: Fishing, Boating, Picnicking, Skating, Bathing, Trapping, Hunting, Smoking, Building Fires, and Any

Acts Tending to Pollute the Waters or to Injure the Property are PROHIBITED. Violators will be PROSECUTED."

But walking is permitted here, as long as you don't wander off the road. It is one of the few places anywhere on the 13,000-acre reservoir property, other than public highways, where even walking is allowed. The road runs below the dam and provides access to a control building. In 1 mile, this road will take you to the far (western) end of the dam and beside the reservoir spillway. Because there is virtually no reservoir business conducted on weekends, the road is ideal for walkers and joggers.

Almost as soon as you begin your walk, you can see that the area was farmed before being taken for the reservoir in 1915. Stone walls still march across the hills, and there are several abandoned roadways visible in the forest, including one that crosses a small brook on a stone bridge just to the left of your road. Six entire villages as well as numerous farms vanished when the land was turned into a reservoir.

In less than ½ mile, you reach a road junction. A turn to the right would take you out to RI 12 at the eastern end of the dam. This is the route that many walkers take after crossing the dam. A turn left, downhill, however, will enable you to walk the full length of the lower road.

Fences line most of the middle segment of the lower road. To the right, high above you, is the dam with RI 12 running along its crest. The entire bank from the highway down to the lower road is grass, a great place for robins and similar birds. At one point, you'll reach a long set of stairs that run from your road all the way up to the old gatehouse at the center of the dam. Usually, the steps are blocked with a chain.

When trees again close in on both sides, you are starting the uphill curve toward the highway. Through the trees on the left, you can see the deep channel for the spillway water before seeing the spillway itself. When you reach the highway, at another barway, take a few moments and walk left to a bridge over the spillway. When the reservoir is full, the roar and spray of the falls are worth a bit of lingering.

As you turn back and start walking along the highway across the dam, the view to your left is that of a forested lake. Rocky shorelines and pine and spruce forests give the reservoir a picturesque aura. To your right, far below, is the roadway you walked earlier.

104

You can walk on either side of the highway. Old-fashioned stone walls run the length of the dam on each side, and sandy paths follow the highway on both sides between the walls and the pavement. It is slightly more than ½ mile across the dam, and you will pass the old gatehouse built in 1926 along the way.

At the eastern end of the dam, on the left side, is a large concrete and bronze tribute to Joseph Gainer, who was mayor of Providence when the reservoir was built. A plaque states that water storage was begun in 1925 and distribution of the water started a year later. Some walkers park here and make the shortest dam-and-lower-road circuit by way of the shortcut road you passed earlier. The shortcut runs off the right side of the highway nearly across from the monument. Walking only this loop would make a hike of just over 1 mile.

If you take this short connector to the lower road and return to your car, your walk will be about 2 miles. If you continue eastward on RI 12 to RI 116, then turn right and walk to your car, you will travel about 2½ miles. However, I like to make the trip a bit longer, so I turn left just beyond the monument on a road that follows the reservoir out to RI 116. There is no signpost on this road but this was part of the original Scituate Avenue, a name now used on the straightened RI 12.

An earthen dike runs along the left side of this road and a dense woods is on the right. There is little traffic and sometimes the road seems to be paved in acorns and pine cones, but you will immediately know this road is open to traffic, unlike the dam's lower road, because you will again see litter that, happily, is absent on the lower road.

Shortly after passing a small cemetery on your right, you will reach RI 116. Turn right. A boggy area complete with skunk cabbage and other swamp plants will be on your right and a woods filled with ledges and stones will be on the left.

In a matter of minutes, you will reach RI 12. Cross it and head downhill toward your car. Chances are the robins will still be in the grassy field where you began.

26. Durfee Hill

A stroll to Killingly Pond on the border of Rhode Island and Connecticut

Hiking distance: 9 miles
Hiking time: 4-4½ hours

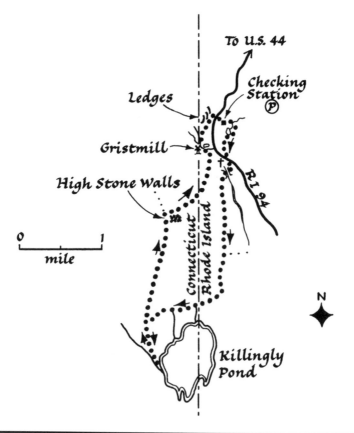

WALKING FROM DURFEE HILL TO KILLINGLY
Pond and back is a 9-mile stroll, one of the longest in this book, but it seems far shorter. Not only is it easy and relatively level, but there is enough to see along the way to keep you interested.

The walk begins in a state management area, circles around a small pond, then wanders for miles through a superb forest before reaching Killingly Pond, most of which is in Connecticut. The return trip, also through forest, follows a different trail that visits a unique network of stone walls, then curls around for a look at a gristmill before finishing up along a high, rugged ledge.

A note of caution, however: This is not a blazed trail in the usual sense of the word, and the numerous side paths make it confusing. It may be best to make this walk with a hiking club that knows the area before attempting it on your own. The only markers are tiny blue ribbons tied to bushes and saplings along the route. At the present, they adequately show the way, but such ribbons are far from permanent.

ACCESS

To reach the start, drive U.S. 44 in Glocester almost to the Connecticut line, turning south on RI 94 across from Bowdish Reservoir. Follow RI 94 1.3 miles to a hunter checking station, on the left, in the Durfee Hill Management Area. You can park here.

TRAIL

Although the vast forest would make this a pleasing walk in autumn, the area teems with hunters then. Instead, go in spring or early summer. The abundance of evergreen trees makes it a charming walk in winter as well, although this section of Rhode Island receives more snow than most areas, sometimes too much for enjoyable walking.

From the parking area, look over the surrounding countryside. Below and to the right, as you face the station building, lies a small pond. You begin by circling this pond, going left on a faint lane in front of the building. It runs downhill, past the small fields planted for the benefit of wildlife.

As you near the pond, watch closely for a path going to the left into the forest, crossing a brook on a pile of rocks. You then go slightly uphill as you curl around the pond, which is all but out of sight because of the dense hemlocks. At a junction in the trail, where you see a sign saying "Safety Zone," turn left, going down a ravine. In minutes, you emerge on RI 94.

Turn left and walk a short distance, passing a small cemetery on your right. Reenter the woods on your right at the beginning of a guard rail near an electrical pole with the number 92 on it. The trail enters the forest at an angle, then turns right and drops downhill.

You step over one tiny brook, then cross a larger stream on a dilapidated wooden bridge of which little remains other than the support logs. The trail here is somewhat rocky but easy to walk. Azaleas and laurel brighten the route when in bloom but the dominant tree is the hemlock. Hemlocks of all sizes occur so often throughout this hike that some hiking clubs refer to this route as the Hemlock Trail.

At a path junction, turn right (the way left goes only a short distance before leaving state property at a stream). At the next junction, about 3 miles from your start, turn right on a narrow gravel road. It soon turns to dirt but is easy and open. You enter Connecticut along this lane and are walking parallel to Killingly Pond. Ignore the cutoffs to the left — they are on private property — and enjoy this quiet, shady segment where red squirrels far outnumber people.

After the lane returns to gravel and you can see Connecticut state property signs on both sides, begin looking for a lane to the left, barred with green metal posts and a metal pole. There are similar posts on a lane going right; this will be your return route.

Go left on the open dirt lane. It runs downhill to a gravel road, which you can take a short distance left to the pond. The pond is 4½ miles from your start, the halfway mark, and is an excellent place for a lunch break. Although undeveloped, it is a scenic, popular place for fishing, swimming, picnicking, and small-boat activity.

When ready to resume walking, go back up the gravel road and the dirt lane. Pass the green-posted barway, cross the roadway you walked earlier and follow the other open path, now straight ahead. If unsure of the way, you can retrace your route but this path is well-worn, used by bikers as well as hikers. Look for the blue ribbons.

Again, you have to disregard cutoff trails and stay on the main path. For much of this segment, there are low stone walls on both sides. The walking is easy and pleasant. There are fewer hemlocks here, rather a good mixture of hardwoods, including a great many young chestnuts. Unfortunately, there are several areas here with deep ruts that often fill with water, so you may get muddy feet during wet weather.

At a Y fork in the trail, bear right. The path makes a sweeping curve right, then swings back left. Soon, you'll notice a network of unusually high stone walls, running at what seems like erratic angles on both sides of the trail. Take a few minutes to check them out; they apparently are from a long-vanished barn and livestock compound.

Just beyond the walls, the trail makes a sharp right and then weaves downhill to a gravel road. To the right, just a few yards away, you can see a highway. This is RI 94 and, if tired, you can take it to the left back to your car, making a walk of close to 8 miles.

You would be missing two of the highlights of the trip, however. Instead, turn left on the gravel road, then quickly right on another gravel road that crosses a bridge. Here, you can look over a former gristmill just left of the road. Although the cottage is still rented out occasionally to hunters or fishermen, you can go around and beneath it to examine the stone dam under the bridge and the stone sluice that still brings water through the lower part of the building. The waterwheel is gone but one of the large round millstones is lying in the cottage's yard.

Next, take the road uphill, past a house on the right, until reaching the first lane going off into the woods on the right. Follow this lane, carpeted with pine needles, as it goes uphill, then around the right side of a swampy area.

Watch closely for a narrow side trail going off to the left. Again, look for the blue ribbons. This side path follows an impressive, rugged rock ledge that looms above on your left nearly all the way out to RI 94. When you reach the highway, turn left and you'll be back at your car in 0.2 mile.

27. Walkabout Trail

Three choices of loops in one walk to ponds, hemlock groves, and a wildlife marsh

Hiking distance: 7½ miles
Hiking time: 3½-4 hours

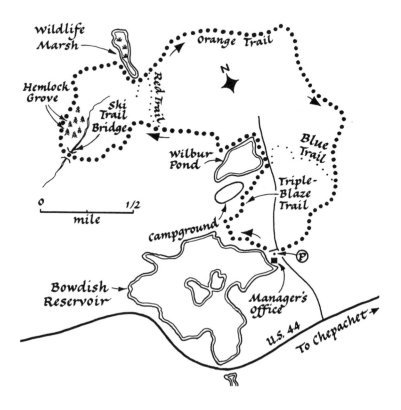

THE WALKABOUT TRAIL HAS UNDERGONE SEV-
eral changes in recent years — some good and some bad, from a
hiker's point of view — but it is still among the more popular trails
and can be a delight under the right conditions.

Although a sign at its start, near Bowdish Reservoir in the Glocester portion of the George Washington Management Area, continues
to list the three walking loops as 2, 6, and 8 miles, all are a bit
shorter now and there is no longer a plant-identifying nature trail
at one end.

The three trails begin and end together, and still take you beside
a campground, around a couple of ponds, through dense woodland,
and across boggy areas. When you take the widest loop, the 8-mile
circuit described here, you also wander through one of the most
impressive hemlock groves in Rhode Island and visit a wildlife
marsh.

The Walkabout was cut and named by Australian sailors back in
1965, while their ship, the Perth, was in dry dock in Newport. The
name refers to the wanderings of the Australian aborigines.

ACCESS

To reach the trailhead, take U.S. 44 to the George Washington
Camping Area, about 4½ miles west of Chepachet. Turn right onto
the campground road and continue 0.3 mile until you reach a lane
that runs by the park office on the left. Turn and park along this
wide lane.

TRAIL

I've walked these trails in all seasons and feel, without a doubt,
that autumn is best. Because the trail runs so near a pond, and
crosses lowlands, it is likely to be quite muddy or even flooded in
spring. Summer's problems include the crowds from the
campground and beach, as well as mosquitoes in the boggy areas,
and the rocky terrain can make water walking very treacherous,
although the hemlocks and pines are stunning in snow.

It is difficult to find any drawbacks in fall. I walked the trail once
on a sparkling Saturday morning in October, and went more than
7 miles without seeing another person. Chickadees and other birds
accompanied me all the way. There were chipmunks and red squir-

rels busy in the trees, and the colors of the mixed forest ranged from gold and orange to deep green. Also, there are far fewer campers (the official camping season runs from May 1 to September 30) and no fees are charged for entering the area in fall.

The trails begin behind a large sign near the beach of Bowdish Reservoir. The 8-mile loop is blazed in orange, the 6-mile loop in red, and the 2-mile loop in blue. Following the brightly painted triple blazes, you start by walking the reservoir shoreline, a pleasant stroll through laurel, pine, and hemlock with frequent cutoffs to rocky points jutting into the water. There are footbridges over some low spots, the first of many plank bridges you'll find on this trail. The path soon swings right, skirting the campground. This is where the walks were shortened when the trail was rerouted during an expansion of the camping area.

You'll see some white marks on trees near the campground, but they have nothing to do with the Walkabout. Stay with the triple blazes as the trail runs along a woods lane briefly. When you reach a gravel road, note that only the blue trail continues straight ahead; the orange and red routes swing left into the forest, starting the circuit around Wilbur Pond.

It's a busy pond in summer but tranquil and picturesque in fall. The trail, after some up-and-down scrambling, runs at the pond's very edge and this is where you may have to detour in high water. You circle about half of the pond before the trail breaks away and goes uphill to the right into an open, pleasant woodland.

In slightly less than ½ mile, you reach the sign indicating the red loop turns off to the right. This shortcut passes numerous stone walls and rock piles that show the area was once farmland, and then crosses a brook before rejoining the orange loop. The red trail, which misses the best hemlock groves and the wildlife marsh, is considerably shorter than the advertised 6 miles; probably under 5 miles.

Remain on the orange trail, which my pedometer now clocks at 7½ miles, and you soon reach a number of gravel lanes (popular in winter as snowmobile trails). At most crossings, you'll find a bench and trash barrel, more recent improvements. When you cross the third roadway in about ¼ mile, you find a sign barring "unauthorized vehicles" on what starts out as a wide, grassy lane.

It winds downhill into a dense hemlock area, and the trail quickly narrows. Trees tower above you on both sides and the thick, ever-green foliage casts a deep, permanent shadow over the trail. For a brief period, you'll walk on a wide, smooth path that crosses a rocky brook on a superb bridge; this is part of a cross-country ski trail that begins at Peck Pond in nearby Pulaski State Park.

Just beyond the bridge, an orange arrow painted on a tree indicates your trail swings right into the brush. The path is narrow here and there are several fallen trees to climb past. For a considerable distance, the trail runs parallel to a gravel road and then crosses it, leading to a section much easier to walk, even though you are at times returning to rocky footing.

In about ½ mile, you cross another road, and almost immediately reach the wildlife marsh. Trees at the water's edge offer veils from which you can observe the marsh inhabitants, mainly muskrats, swallows (in summer), kingfishers and the colorful wood ducks that are lured by the wooden nesting boxes installed on poles above the water. The trail crosses the earthen dam built to create the marsh and offers a good opportunity to pause and take a good look.

As soon as you cross the dike, the trail splits. Go left (the path to the right is unmarked) and you'll soon meet the red-blazed trail coming in from the right. In another ½ mile you will cross your final gravel road and, before long, drop into a lovely but wet area of laurel, hemlocks, and moss. Here, you may have to pick your way, even in autumn, by stepping on exposed roots.

When you climb out of the damp section, you are very close to rejoining the blue trail you left miles earlier, and from the intersection it is only ½ mile, to the left, back to your car.

28. Buck Hill

*A "three-state" walk through
an area abundant in wildlife*

Hiking distance: 4.7 miles
Hiking time: 2½-3 hours

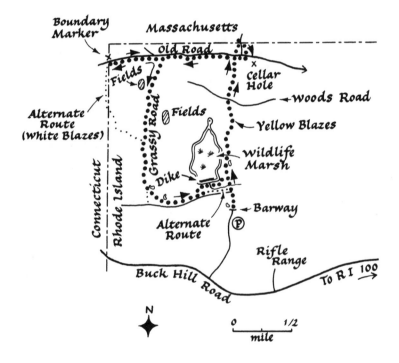

BUCK HILL IS ONE OF THE PLACES TO GO TO IF you want to combine walking with wildlife watching. It offers plenty of both.

The Buck Hill State Management Area is in Burrillville, the extreme northwest corner of the state. Management of this forest has resulted in an abundance of wildlife, both waterfowl and upland game, along with all the songbirds and small animals that such areas attract.

The walk described here runs beside a man-made marsh, through rocky woodlots and along a grassy road that passes numerous management fields, meadows, and small ponds. In the 4.7-mile loop, you'll also step briefly into Massachusetts and Connecticut, so you can boast of walking in three states in your 2½-hour ramble.

What wildlife you see depends on when you visit, and how observant — and lucky — you are. Ducks, owls, hawks, grouse, quail, pheasants, wild turkeys, deer, foxes, rabbits, squirrels, woodchucks, raccoons, and numerous other creatures inhabit Buck Hill, as well as dozens of varieties of songbirds.

ACCESS

To reach the unmarked entrance, take RI 100 north from Pascoag to Buck Hill Road and turn left. Watch your odometer; the entrance is 2.3 miles from the turnoff. You will pass a fire tower and a road for a Boy Scout Camp on your left, then a rifle range on the right, before reaching the gravel access road, also on the right.

During most of the year, you can drive only ⅓ mile before being stopped at a barway. On the right, you will see signs warning of a rifle range; stay out of that area. During hunting season — fall and early winter — you can continue driving the management roads, but that is Buck Hill's busiest time and the wrong time for walking.

Moving the parking area away from the marsh has made this a slightly longer walk than previously, but it is more pleasant now. Not only is there more wildlife, but also the trails and lanes are more open and easier to walk.

TRAIL

From the barway, walk straight ahead on the gravel road. You will see other roads and the first of many tiny ponds with nesting boxes for wood ducks. At an intersection, you'll see white blazes along a road coming from the left; that is your return route. Yellow blazes appear on the road going straight ahead. Follow them and in a few minutes you will reach the large marsh, where there are many more duck houses and hundreds of skeletons of trees killed when a dike was put up to create the marsh. It's an intriguing place, and sometimes a bit eerie, particularly in early morning, when mist rises from the water, and in evening, when shadows loom.

After taking time to look over the marsh, which usually is alive with swallows, blackbirds, flycatchers, and waxwings, in addition to ducks, follow the yellow blazes around to the right and into the woods. Here the path narrows considerably and the surface is very rocky. In places, you can still see a bit of orange paint on some of the trees; years ago the blazes were the brightest orange available.

In less than 1 mile from your start, you'll reach a woods road. Follow the blazes directly across it. The next section has larger trees, some laurel undergrowth and a number of stone walls, reminders that this was once farmland. At 1.4 miles, you emerge on another road, this one an ancient thoroughfare lined by stone walls. Again, the yellow-blazed path goes directly over it. If you continue following the blazes, you'll reach the state line border in about 1/10 mile, and you can say you walked to Massachusetts.

Retrace your steps back to the old wagon road, turn left (east) and walk just a few yards and you can find the cellar hole at what is supposed to be the site of the area's first homesteader. In recent years, much of the brush around the cellar has been cleared away and it is now much easier to find. It's on a small knoll, just off the right side of the road.

From here, turn around and walk back down the road, past the yellow-marked path you took earlier. There are no blazes along the road but none are needed. It is still an open, easy-to-walk roadway. Soon, you reach a wide, grassy lane on the left. This leads to the management fields, but if you want to say you've walked to Connecticut, stay on the old road. You can walk the grassy lane later; the stroll to the state boundary and back will add only about ¾ mile to your hike.

When the road curves right, toward an open field, look straight ahead, beyond a fallen tree. You can see the outline of the overgrown road in the woods, and a narrow footpath will keep you going west.

The path is soon joined by a motorcycle trail coming in from the right and then is wider as it goes downhill. Just beyond a point where a brook runs under a flat-stone bridge on the road, where a white-blazed cycle path crosses the road, look for the boundary marker. It is an upright field stone with "RI" chiseled into one side, "C" on the other.

You could take the white-marked trail, to the left, but you would miss nearly 1 mile of the grassy lane, and consequently, much of the wildlife that makes Buck Hill special. Therefore, I recommend backtracking to the lane you passed earlier, now on your right.

Immediately, you'll see a small pond, on your right, with the inevitable wood duck house. There are similar ponds ahead, and numerous small clearings — fields cut from the forest. Some are planted in grains, some are left in meadows. In spring, it's not unusual to hear a quail whistling or a pheasant crowing from these fields, and if you happen by at the right time of day — morning or evening — you might see a deer or fox here. I've also seen woodchucks and rabbits on the trail itself, and at each pool you are likely to find deer tracks and raccoon footprints.

Each field is screened from the lane by trees, and each has an entrance road that enables you to take a look. However, return to the main lane each time. After you have walked nearly 1 mile on the lane, and about 3.7 miles in all, you'll see the white-blazed trail coming in from the right. You'll have the blazes with you the rest of the way back to the gravel road where you began.

(When the lane makes a sweeping curve to the left, you could take a narrow path straight ahead into the woods. It joins another old road which runs downhill to the right to the Connecticut line. However, the border is less distinct here and the road comes out at the rear of a farm on private property. This side jaunt would add ½ mile to your walk.)

Before reaching the gravel road, the grassy lane becomes a sandy woods road that curves considerably. Be sure to look for a narrow path on the left; it leads to the earthen dike at the marsh you saw earlier. If you miss the path, go out to the gravel road and turn left. The dike is a grassy ridge that offers an excellent view of the swamp, and it's the perfect place for a rest stop before heading back to the car.

29. Black Hut

A quiet walk in the woods of Northern Rhode Island

Hiking distance: 6 miles
Hiking time: 2½-3 hours

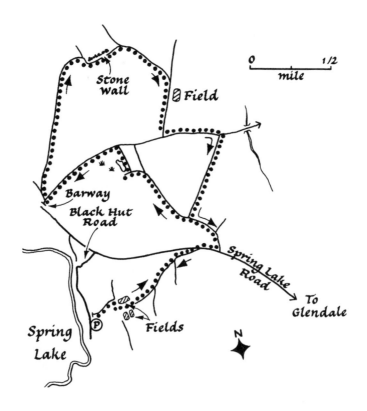

IF YOU ARE LOOKING FOR AN EASY, QUIET WOODS walk, give Black Hut a try. Here, you can roam for miles with little chance of running into other hikers, and maybe not see any other people at all.

The Black Hut Management Area in Burrillville is one of the more overlooked public forests in Rhode Island. It draws some hunters in autumn and early winter, and occasionally trail bikers use the access roads, but for most of the year the 1,300-acre forest is virtually forgotten. Just the kind of place many walkers like.

This walk is pleasant but unspectacular. You won't find high rock ledges here or many historical attractions, but you need not worry about rocky footing or strenuous climbing. For the most part, you simply stroll through hardwood groves. There are several visits to fields planted for wildlife and a stop by a delightful little marsh hidden far back in the woods. The observant may find a great deal of wildlife on this walk.

A note of caution: Although Black Hut is crisscrossed with numerous roads, lanes, and paths, there are no marked hiking trails. So care must be taken to keep from wandering off in the wrong direction. The route described here is just under 6 miles but can be easily shortened or lengthened by taking alternate routes.

ACCESS

Black Hut lies northwest of the village of Glendale. Take RI 102 north from Chepachet or south from Slatersville. From Glendale, take Spring Lake Road northwest for 1.2 miles to Black Hut Road. Turn left, driving by the cluster of houses along the shore of Spring Lake. About ½ mile along Black Hut Road, you will find a parking area on the left, at the foot of a chain-barred gravel lane that runs uphill into the woods.

TRAIL

Following the gravel road, you quickly reach an open field, where grain is usually planted for the benefit of the deer and other animals in the area. Go to the right along the edge of the field, then follow a lane that curves left, running beside two more open fields. Pheasants, woodchucks, doves, and quail often can be seen in these fields.

Beyond the fields, the lane gradually swings left, running downhill through a good mixture of hardwoods, mostly maples, oaks, and birches, with numerous young chestnuts crowding the trail. Mountain laurel is thick here as well, adding much color when blooming in June. You will pass two cutoff paths in this area, going to the right. They would take you through an extensive forest, but they leave state property, so walking them is not recommended.

As you follow the lane downhill beyond the fields, you will pass several damp areas and a seasonal brook will appear on your left. Here, the lane is decorated with ferns and you will walk through a beech grove. Bird song — thrushes, warblers, wrens — is likely to accompany you.

Shortly after the brook cuts across your lane, you'll see a row of hemlocks on the left. They shield a house and other buildings. Here, the trail splits once more. Again, go left, and in a few yards you will emerge on a paved roadway. This is Spring Lake Road, which you drove earlier. The bulk of this walk lies on the opposite side of the road.

Take the road to the right about 1/10 mile and look for a grassy lane running into the woods on the left. This lane is almost opposite a Black Hut Management Area sign.

In another 1/10 mile, the lane forks. Go left, then left again at the next fork. Throughout this area, the walking is dry and easy. When you pass an area where there has been some tree cutting, look for a cutoff to the left. It is narrower than the main lane but well-worn from use by bikers.

Take the cutoff and you will quickly find yourself on a grassy bank above the wildlife marsh. Spend a few minutes on the earthen dike, from where you can watch the swallows swooping over the water and perhaps see ducks, herons, or other water birds.

When ready to resume walking, take the woods road that runs around the right side of the marsh. It will pass several tiny clearings being used as wildlife fields, then emerge at a T intersection with a larger, more-used road.

This is the main access road in this area. Go left on it, uphill, until reaching an orange-painted barway. If you wish, you can pass the barway and go left on Spring Lake Road back to your car. To continue the 6-mile route, however, look for a narrow footpath going into the bushes on the right, just before you reach the barway.

The path soon opens into a comfortable trail, and just as soon, forks. Take the right fork. For ½ mile, you stroll through second-growth hardwoods where ferns, laurel, blueberries, and ladyslippers are thriving. At another trail intersection, where the cyclists usually turn left, go right, curling around the end of a tumbledown stone wall.

This path, once a woods road but seldom used now, follows the stone wall downhill. It is overgrown and damp in places, but it takes you away from most cycle traffic and turns you back toward the forest interior. When you reach a clearing where the lane bends left, be careful. Instead of turning left, cross the clearing and look for a similarly overgrown lane at the far corner.

For about ⅓ mile, you walk this fern-choked lane, which ends at an open, grassy roadway. Go right, passing a cutoff to a field on the left, until the next intersection, which is a segment of the main access road you walked earlier. This time, turn left (a right would take you back toward the marsh).

These roads are delightful. Level and shady, they make you want to linger. Near here, on one June walk, I dallied for some time watching a mother grouse go through her broken-wing act in trying to distract attention away from her brood of downy youngsters.

Don't get too caught up in reverie, however; the next turn is easy to miss. Look for several large rocks atop an embankment on the right side of the roadway. If you reach a bridge and stream, you've gone about 100 yards to far. You'll have to climb the embankment to find the wide but little-worn path.

This is a connector that takes you back toward Spring Lake Road. You will have to cross one boggy area and a low ridge before joining the lane you walked earlier. A left turn and a short walk takes you out to Spring Lake Road. The remainder of your hike is a retracing of your first mile, going up the damp lane, past the fields and back down to your car.

30. Diamond Hill

*A steep climb to the top,
and an easy downhill stroll*

Distance: 2 miles
Walking time: 1½ hours

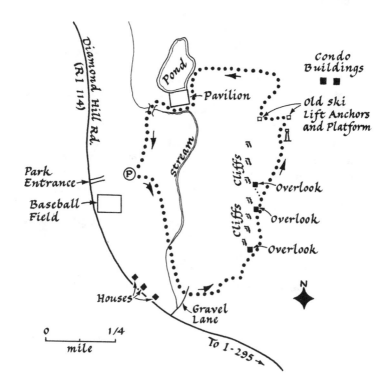

WALKING THE DIAMOND HILL TRAIL HAS CHANGED
several times in recent years, and each change has reduced the mileage considerably. Still, this park in Rhode Island's northeastern corner remains attractive; it's still well worth a visit.

Previously, both sides of steep, rocky Diamond Hill sported skiing operations, and a hiking trail crossed the hill's summit, curled around a reservoir, and wandered into Massachusetts. It was a challenging walk that tested the hiker's woodsmanship and physical stamina.

When the ski businesses fell apart, the state-owned side of the hill was developed into a multi-faceted park. The opposite slope—formerly Ski Valley—was developed in another way. It now is crowded with condominiums.

So this walk through Diamond Hill State Park is barely two miles, but it continues to provide considerable charm. It begins with the challenge of a climb to the top of a rocky cliff that offers panoramic views of the region, then ends with a stroll through a park that adds its own attractions at all times of year.

Be prepared to spend some time enjoying the park after your walk. There are free concerts in summer, spectacular foliage in autumn, sledding and skating in winter, and trout fishing and kite-flying in spring. The walk described here will take less than two hours, but bring along a picnic or sled or a kite or a fishing rod, and a visit to Diamond Hill can easily wile away most of a day.

ACCESS

Take I-295 into Cumberland, exit on RI 114 (Diamond Hill Road), and follow the road 4 miles to Diamond Hill State Park, which is on the right. It doesn't matter which part of the large parking lot you choose; you will begin by walking to the right and return from the left.

TRAIL

At the right front section of the parking lot, you'll find a line of trees bordering a small stream. Walk along this edge of the lot to the right, going through an auxiliary parking lot (usually barred). The stream will be on your left, and you'll see a baseball field on your right.

Where the gravel ends, the stream cuts across your path, but you can cross the water on large pipes. You are now following an old railroad bed (the tracks were removed long ago) so the trail is straight and level. Continue, while passing behind a few homes, until reaching a gravel lane coming in from RI 114 on the right.

Towering above you on the left is a 150-foot cliff. Several trails go up the rocks, which are marred by decades of graffiti, but look for a small, triangular sign that indicates the Warner Trail. This spot was the southern terminus of the long trail once maintained by the Appalachian Mountain Club that ran from here to Canton, Massachusetts.

Take the well-worn trail to the rim. It's a relatively steep and strenuous climb, but not really very dangerous, and you reach the top in minutes. You'll still see a few of the metal discs that formerly marked the trail, but these days dabs of orange paint on rocks and trees are the blazes to look for.

On the rim, take some time to enjoy the view. Spread out below is Diamond Hill village, and beyond are hills and forests. Also, you can often watch mountain climbers using this headwall to practice their rappelling techniques.

The orange trail runs along the rim to several rock outlooks, but other paths follow easier parallel routes through the woods a few yards back from the edge. Take your pick.

When you reach a large water tower, installed for the condominium project below you on the right, the trail becomes more difficult to follow. Go around the left side of the tower, and you will reach two huge concrete foundations that once served as anchors for the ski lift lines. From these foundations, take a path to the left for several yards to another concrete platform. This was the spot where skiers dismounted for their runs down the hill. Now saplings and young trees are thriving here; they nearly obscure the view.

The orange-blazed trail continues going to the right, through a grove of young birches, until it reaches an old gravel lane that provides a look at the Ski Valley condominium complex and the reservoir beyond. At this point, the old Warner Trail plunged downhill through the forest, but since it is now severed at numerous points by roads, homes, and private property, hikers should stop looking for the discs and orange blazes.

Instead, follow the gravel lane as it curls from the summit to the left, descending toward the grassy slopes of the state park. You'll have to swing around the end of a fence, but in moments you are in an area ideal for sledding or kite-flying, and a few more strides will take you to the pond and pavilion where Sunday concerts are held in summer. The trout stream is behind and beyond the pavilion, and picnic facilities are all around. You are now ready for the second half of your day in the park.

31. Lincoln Woods

A leisurely park stroll around a picturesque pond

Hiking distance: 3 miles
Hiking time: 1½-2 hours

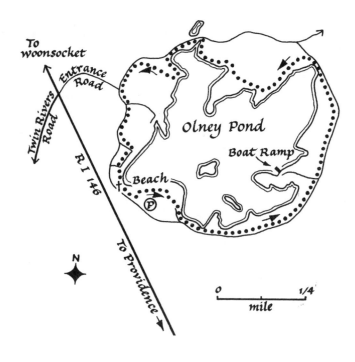

LINCOLN WOODS IS A LARGE, OLD PARK CLOSE

to Rhode Island's population centers, but it is often overlooked by walkers, particularly those who prefer the solitude of so-called wilderness areas. Such people are missing a good thing.

On this easy loop around the park's central feature, picturesque Olney Pond, you will stroll just under 3 miles. You can walk a road all the way, if you wish, or swing through forest on several occasions. You can try your hand at fishing, take time for a picnic, or even end your walk with a refreshing swim. There are a great many other paths and trails through the woods, but none are blazed and sorting them out can be confusing, so walking around the pond is the recommended route.

The park is a busy place, especially in summer, but in spring and autumn there is plenty of room for walking. You are not likely to see much wildlife, although ducks and songbirds are common, as are squirrels, chipmunks, and muskrats. And there is the sport of people-watching. Along your route you will meet joggers, picnickers, bicyclists, and families strolling with small children. In areas, there will be fishermen, horsemen, orienteering competitors, and sunbathers.

ACCESS

The park is in Lincoln, almost within sight of Providence, Pawtucket, North Providence, and Central Falls. Access from both the north and south is provided by RI 146 via Twin Rivers Road. In summer, a per-vehicle fee is charged for entering, but there is no charge from Labor Day to Memorial Day.

From the entrance, go to the right, past the first parking lot, to the beach area and its complex of modern buildings. The beach, food concessions, and restrooms (open only in summer) make this a good place to end a walk.

TRAIL

After parking in one of the nearby lots, cross a bridge near the buildings, then begin the hike by following a walkway of fine gravel around to the right. You'll be passing an open playing field on the right and large trees along the shoreline on your left.

In minutes, you will be on a paved road at the water's edge and climbing one of the many inclines on this route. The road alternately goes down to the very edge of the pond, then climbs many feet above it. In all but summer, you can see the water through the trees virtually throughout the walk. The pond is the star of this show, its rocky shoreline, wooded islands, and numerous coves all pleasing to the eyes in every season.

At a gravel roadway to the left, leading to a boat ramp, you'll have gone about 0.7 mile. Just beyond, the paved road climbs another hill and curls away from the pond briefly. Just off the road, to the right, are a string of houses, reminders of just how close this park lies to residential areas.

When the road drops downhill again, you reach a concrete wall and small dam, invariably crowded with fishermen. This is approximately the halfway point of the walk. Just beyond the dam, you can leave the pavement, swinging left into the woods. There are numerous paths here, but there is little chance of getting lost. The pond is on one side and the road on the other. The best rule is to follow the shore.

You will reach a spot where it seems there are two ponds separated by a narrow strip of land. This is actually a dead-end point; stay to the right and resume walking the shoreline. There are huge, jagged boulders that might make you forget you're in such a "city park" — unless you can smell hot dogs being grilled at the picnic tables along the road.

The path snakes between the boulders and emerges on the road almost directly across from a very small pond. Turn left and follow the road a short distance until it curves right. You can go left, through a picnic area beside inviting rocks that offer lovely views of the lake. Again, you can follow the shoreline, but in 100 yards or so, you will reach a boggy area that will make a right turn through the woods and out to the road necessary.

Soon you pass the entrance road on your right, and then a fishing access road on your left. Remain on the main park road until reaching a parking area in a grove of tall pines.

Walk along the rear of the parking lot, then cut across a grassy slope where there are many picnic tables and a restroom. Take a few moments to look over an ancient cemetery surrounded by a thick stone wall. This is the resting place of the Olney family, for whom the pond was named. Some of the tombstones date from the 1700s.

Walk down the slope to the water's edge, then follow a wide path to the right. It takes you around the final corner of the pond to the beach. Your walk will be finished, and it will be time for a plunge or a picnic.

32. Dame Farm-Snake Den

*One walk back in time to view
a vanishing lifestyle and another
to see rattlesnake dens*

Hiking distance: 3½ miles
Hiking time: 2½ hours

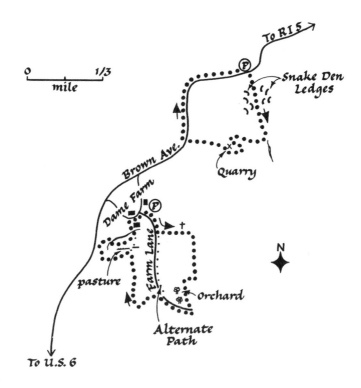

THESE TWO WALKS, ALMOST IN THE SHADOW OF
Providence and the metropolitan population, remain among the
farthest removed in feeling and tempo. Snake Den State Park and
its featured attraction, Dame Farm, lie within a few miles of
thousands of people, yet they belong to another era, a simpler time
when each family formed its own community. The Dame Farm
walk, in particular, gives you a look back at Rhode Island farming
— a vanishing lifestyle.

I split these walks into separate strolls, but they could be walked
together if you don't mind walking about 1 mile on a paved roadway.
Together, they total slightly more than 3½ miles. Hike them sepa-
rately (which means moving your car) and you will walk about 3
miles.

Of the two, the Dame Farm walk is easily the more popular and
interesting — wandering around a working farm and its fields and
orchards, as well as traveling a woods path with signs indicating
what role each section played during the farm's heyday.

The second trail is, for the most part, simply a pleasant forest
walk but it takes you among the rugged rock ledges where the
famed rattlesnakes, for which Snake Den Park was named, supposedly lived. I recommend you take your time walking the farm
paths first, then if you still have ambition, visit the ledge area. The
best ledges are near Brown Avenue, where you will be parking, so
you can take a look at the ledges and return to your car, or walk
the entire Snake Den circuit I describe here.

ACCESS

To reach the park, which stretches along the east side of Brown
Avenue in Johnston, follow U.S. 6 west 2 miles from I-295 and
turn right onto Brown Avenue. You will reach Dame Farm, on the
right, in 1.6 miles. From northern Rhode Island, take RI 5 1 mile
west of the U.S. 44–RI 5 junction in Greenville, then turn right
onto Brown Avenue. The farm is 1.5 miles on the left.

Park near the left end of the barn, where you will see the start
of a farm lane. Also, you can pick up (for 25 cents) a map of the
trail from a blue mailbox beside the lane.

TRAIL

The trail starts along the lane, but quickly swings left through a field to a small family cemetery. Because this is still a working farm — the livelihood of the Dame Family — if you visit during growing season and the fields are planted in corn or wheat, it would be prudent to skip the swing left and remain on the lane. You can walk through the fields after harvest in fall or during the winter.

After passing the cemetery and another tiny graveyard, which is little more than a pile of old tombstones now, the trail goes through a narrow woodlot and emerges in what was the Dames' orchard. About three-fourths of the trees are gone now, many victims of the 1938 hurricane and others felled by storms in succeeding years. If you stayed on the farm lane, it also will lead to this orchard.

Numbered signs at various places (ponds, rock piles, woodlots) point out the role each area played a hundred years ago, when the farm was nearly self-sufficient. They provide an interesting insight into what farm life was at that time. Unfortunately, in several places only the numbers remain; the descriptive signs are missing.

A note of caution: If you walk this area in autumn, you could run into hunters in the woodlots around the orchard. It can be less than relaxing to know there is a shotgun-toting person prowling through the brush just a few yards away. That might be another good reason to stay on the farm lane until you reach stop number 11, where the trail turns into the hillside forest directly behind the barn. There, hunting is not allowed.

The woods trail, blazed in white, curves back toward the buildings. At one point, you'll have to squeeze through a narrow opening between two trees (a barbed wire fence prevents going around), then you'll cross an aptly named boulder field before reaching a pasture that overlooks the farm.

Until recently, this pasture, which features a magnificent, 200-year-old oak tree, offered a panoramic view of the entire area, but now many saplings and bushes have sprouted and blocked the view somewhat. The oak still provides an ideal spot for resting, however.

Many people end their walk by strolling through the pasture down to the barn area. The trail, though, swings left through a woodlot, where you'll have to slip between strands of another barbed wire fence, crosses a brook, and then goes downhill on a rocky slope, where there is another "fat man's squeeze." At this point, on my last visit, I sat on a rock and watched a flock of Canada geese feeding in a harvested corn field.

The trail goes into the field briefly, crosses a brook, and follows the edge of the woods back to the barn. The walk, slightly under 2 miles, takes only 1½ hours, so you may have time to look over the buildings, now listed in the National Registry of Historical Places.

If you want to see the snake dens of Snake Den Park, drive exactly 1 mile east on Brown Avenue, and park where you see a dirt lane going into the forest. It's a short walk to the ledges that loom above the lane on both sides. There hasn't been a rattlesnake here in many years, but once they supposedly were so thick this wagon road was literally blocked by the writhing reptiles.

Beyond the ledges, the unmarked path continues straight ahead. After passing through a second ravine you'll reach a junction. Go right. You'll walk through a pleasant woods briefly, then break into an open area from which you can see houses along Brown Avenue. Turn left for a few yards and reenter the woods. The path circles an abandoned stone quarry, which has interestingly shaped stone slabs left behind. Unfortunately, this area apparently is the scene of many beer parties and the litter is disturbing. The path follows a lane out to the roadway. Dame Farm is to your left. Your car is about ¾ mile to the right.

33. Osamequin Park

A leisurely stroll through a bird sanctuary

Hiking distance: 1 mile
Hiking time: 1 hour

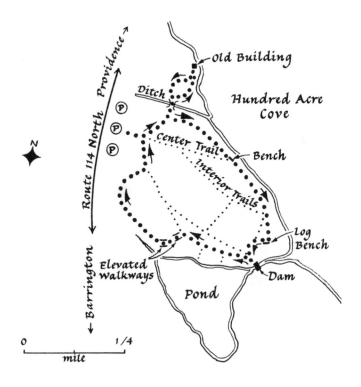

OSAMEQUIN PARK IS A TINY WILDLIFE SANCTUARY
that offers a leisurely stroll in a part of the state better known for
congested traffic, mushrooming development, and all the other
maladies of urban sprawl.

This is a short walk—one mile by the route described here—
and made to order for those more interested in birds and plants than
in chalking up miles. The primary attraction is the wide, marshy
segment of the Barrington River known as Hundred Acre Cove
that forms the eastern boundary of the park. The sanctuary also
includes a brackish pond, wetlands, several thickets and some open
meadows. All are filled with birds.

Osamequin Park, named for an Indian chief who sold land in the
area to colonists in 1653, is owned by the town of Barrington and
maintained by the town and the Barrington Garden Club. A separate and smaller segment of the park lies about half a mile farther
north of the main sanctuary.

ACCESS

Osamequin park is on Route 114 North, better known as the
Wampanoag Trail, at the northern end of Barrington. Drivers coming from the north (Providence and East Providence) should look
for the Zion Bible Institute exit on the right, then take the next
opportunity to switch to the northbound lane of the divided highway.
Those coming from the south should travel through Barrington
center and watch for the park about a mile beyond the White Church,
a local landmark. Signs for the refuge and a parking lot are just off
the right shoulder of 114 North.

TRAIL

Walkers have a choice of routes because numerous trails run
through the 42-acre sanctuary. Many visitors take a wide grassy
path from the entrance directly across the park to a wooden bench
beside the river. It's an excellent spot for checking on water birds.

However, to get the most out of a visit to Osamequin, I suggest
making a circular walk that provides access to all of its various ter-
rains and attractions. This route roughly follows the perimeter of
the park and offers numerous vantage points near the water.

A word of caution: while the trails are kept open and clean, they are not marked well in some areas and a new visitor can be confused by the many intersections. Trails are supposed to be marked in red, blue, yellow and green but the blazes are on posts, instead of painted on trees, and a number of posts are missing. Still, getting lost is not a worry in such a small park.

Just a few yards beyond the entrance is the first trail junction, at a bench and a sign in several languages. Go left on a path that curls through a wooded area, over a wooden walkway and then across a footbridge. Below the bridge is a ditch cut back in the 1930s in a mosquito-control project. Its water level rises and drops with the tide.

Beyond the bridge, the path forks. Go right, and in a few minutes you are at the river's edge. Chances are there will be egrets, swans and other birds in the water at any time of year, and the place is often crowded with ducks and geese during spring and fall migrations.

Follow the shore until reaching a small, abandoned cement block building. In this area, you may see people as well as birds wading in the shallow water, searching for shellfish. The clammers come here via a narrow path that runs from a small parking area along the highway.

Start retracing your steps along the shore, then go right at a fork that will take you into a thicket. This is a short trail that ends at the bridge you crossed earlier, but may enable you to see woods birds you might otherwise miss.

After recrossing the bridge and the low walkway, turn left immediately. This path returns you to the river and takes you along the most popular and most picturesque section of the park. In front of you is the cove called, in a park pamphlet, "Rhode Island's most extensive and pristine inland estuarine system." Beyond the marsh area you can see boats and homes. To the right is open water and the White Church on the horizon. Even without birds, it's easy to understand why people linger here.

When ready to resume walking, continue following the shore-line path until it ends at a log bench. Then go inland a few steps to an intersection, turn left, then take another left at the next fork, a four-trail junction. The left fork leads to a dam between the cove and a pond. A narrow trail to the right will provide your first look at the pond, which usually holds an abundance of herons, egrets, sandpipers and other birds, along with muskrats, frogs and turtles.

Return to the four-trail corner and go left. Now there are more

136

markers and you are following the red trail as it weaves through dense thickets along the pond. Several side trails run to the water, although mud and tall reeds sometimes make viewing difficult.

When you reach an elevated walkway, cross it, and then take another walkway that goes through a jungle-like growth of the reeds, called *phragmites*. If you go when the reeds are not at full growth, or if you're tall, you can see most of the pond from the walkway.

By this time, you are back near the highway, and a short walk beyond the walkway will take you to the center trail. At this point, you can return to the parking lot and your car, or take one of the interior trails for more birding.

34. Prudence Island

*Ferry ride and a walk in an
island park through the densest
deer population in Rhode Island*

Hiking distance: 8¼ miles
Hiking time: 4-4½ hours

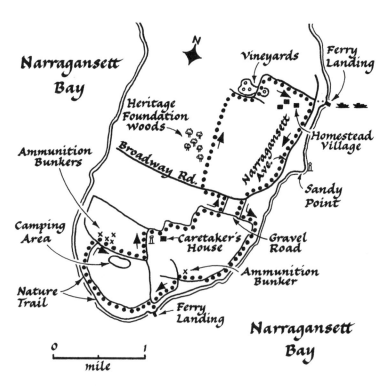

SOLITUDE IS AN OVERRIDING THEME ON PRU-
dence Island. A walk here offers plenty of ocean views, wildlife,
and bits of history, both military and agricultural, but one of the
best aspects is that crowds have not yet discovered this place.

Lying virtually in the center of Narragansett Bay, Prudence Island
is considered the crown jewel in Rhode Island's new Bay Islands
Park System. Both the south and north ends are now public parks.
Much work has been done in both areas in recent years and plans
call for continued improvement that may yet attract boatloads of
visitors, but there seems little chance of Prudence becoming the
bustling, moped-infested resort of a Block Island.

Birding enthusiasts may prefer Prudence's north end, which is
a national estuarine sanctuary that attracts a great many water birds.
However, there are fewer ferry rides available to the north end at
the present — none in spring, fall, or winter — and it is a long
walk to the sanctuary from the regular ferry landing in Homestead.

Therefore, walking the south end and returning through the
center of the island is recommended. This 8¼-mile stroll provides
a look at Homestead, the island's only village; runs through South
Prudence State Park, with its seascapes, new nature trail, and old
military bunkers; wanders through abandoned farmland now pre-
served for deer and other wildlife; and finally goes through the
island's vineyards before returning to Homestead.

ACCESS

The Homestead ferry runs from Bristol on the east side of Narragansett Bay, with several trips each day in summer, fewer in
spring and fall, and one daily in winter. Schedules change frequently
and it is best to check ahead by calling the Prudence Island Navi-
gation Company. The departure point in Bristol is on Thames Street
at the foot of Church Street.

TRAIL

From the landing in Homestead, go left on the first street, Narragansett Avenue, which follows the shoreline past Sandy Point,
another ferry landing that features a small lighthouse. Often, there
are small boats moored near here and flocks of cormorants, gulls,
terns, and other water birds are not uncommon.

Follow the road as it runs uphill, away from the water and out of the village. Where the main road makes a sharp turn right, go straight ahead on a new road (unfinished at this writing). In a short distance, it ends at a gravel road that marks the beginning of state property.

For this walk, turn left, toward the water. Notice a high, barbed wire fence running along the left side of this lane. The fence, which runs a zigzag route all across the island, shows how much land was used by the U.S. Navy in World War II, when this end of the island served as a key point in the defense plans for Narragansett Bay. Now the fence is virtually blanketed by surging wild grape vines and honeysuckle.

The gravel lane soon turns right and follows the shoreline. To the left, you can often see barges, lobster boats, and other craft that use the bay as a working place. Across the water, you can see Mount Hope Bridge to the extreme left, some of the buildings of Portsmouth directly east, and the Newport Bridge to the extreme right.

Birds abound in this section, as the lane is lined with numerous bushes and vines that produce berries. You also are likely to see deer tracks here, and perhaps the deer themselves, as Prudence Island has the densest deer population of any place in New England. Chances of seeing deer depend a great deal on the time of your visit. Mornings and evenings are better than midafternoon; all other seasons are better than midsummer.

The first sign of the old military activity is a concrete boat ramp, now unused, and soon you reach an empty storage building. Here, the lane surface changes to concrete. Shortly, you will pass the first of several underground ammunition bunkers that lie along this route. Closed and barred to the public, each shows only a rounded cement foundation covered with grasses and bushes above ground.

At a crossroads, turn left, toward the water, and walk toward a long ferry dock, where most park visitors and campers land. At an information booth on the dock, pick up a pamphlet for the nature trail, which begins at the dock. The trail consists of numbered posts and you'll need the pamphlet to learn the significance of each post. Most deal with plants, but some also point out historical features or places visible across the water.

From the dock, the nature trail turns left (west) and runs near the shore, passing a pole and platform put up for ospreys. In addition to the abundance of interesting plants along the route, you also have excellent views across the water of Jamestown Island, Quonset Point (a former Navy air station), and Hope Island, as you make your way north.

When the lane intersects a concrete road near another bunker, go right (the lane left follows the shoreline for some distance, then turns inland). You will still be on the nature trail as you walk through a camping area equipped with picnic tables and restrooms and pass several more bunkers.

At the next crossroads, leave the nature trail (it turns right, back toward the park's ferry landing). To the left, you will see a high, rusting water tower. As you walk toward it, notice the open areas cut in the brush as fire breaks. Deer frequently browse at the edge of such clearings.

Just beyond the water tower and a large garage, turn right, following the road as it passes the park caretaker's house. There, the road turns to gravel and you are once more walking beside the old barbed wire boundary. You follow this road nearly 1 mile — sometimes a very dusty mile when there is traffic entering the park — before reaching a dirt roadway on the left. This road (which you should take) is just uphill from the new road you took earlier.

The short dirt road takes you to a paved road (Broadway Road) that connects the east and west sides of the island. Take it, to the left, just a short distance. After cresting a small hill, look for a wooden sign on the right that says "Heritage Foundation of Rhode Island, Visitors Welcome."

Walk along the grassy lane that starts behind the sign. This is one of the most pleasant segments of the entire walk as it runs through one-time farmland that has returned to forest. You pass impressive old stone walls and abandoned apple orchards that provide ideal deer habitat. This area, off-limits to hunters, is your best bet for seeing deer, so walk quietly.

Eventually, you will see a brown house ahead. The lane emerges on a gravel road in front of the house. Turn right, and you soon will be walking beside a high fence that protects a vineyard. Better views of the hundreds of rows of grape vines lie ahead when the road makes a turn left between two large vineyards.

Beyond the vineyards, the road makes a turn right and then becomes pavement. Stay on it, and in minutes you will be walking downhill and passing houses, heading directly for the Homestead ferry landing.

35. Ruecker Wildlife Refuge

A short walk along the Sakonnet River to see fiddler crabs

Hiking distance: 1½ miles
Hiking time: 1½ hours

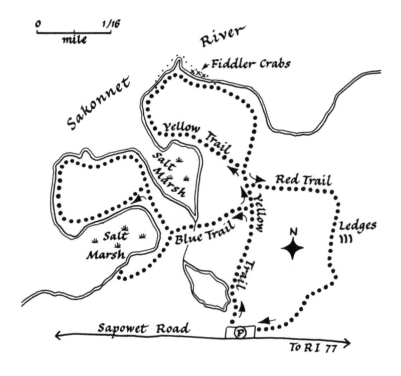

THIS WALK IS A LITTLE JEWEL. LOOPING
through the Emilie Ruecker Wildlife Refuge, it is only 1½ miles
long on an easy-to-walk path. If you like birds and fiddler crabs,
you are likely to be fascinated every step of the way.

The refuge, located on the salty shores of the Sakonnet River in
Tiverton, was a 30-acre farm before the owner, Emilie Ruecker,
donated it to the Rhode Island Audubon Society in 1965. Now,
thanks to its natural attributes — shallow marshes and upland woodlots — and Audubon management, the refuge attracts a wide variety
of bird life, particularly during the spring and fall migrations. The
fiddler crabs and some unusual rock formations add to the attraction,
but for most walkers it is the birds that make the trails of Ruecker
so inviting.

ACCESS

Follow RI 77 south from the village of Tiverton for 3 miles to
Sapowet Road. Turn right and drive ½ mile to the refuge, which
is on the right. The sign and small parking lot are inconspicuous,
so look carefully.

TRAIL

As soon as you leave the car, you start hearing birds. In spring
and early summer, quail whistle from the surrounding pastures and
hayfields, and warblers and catbirds call from within the sanctuary's
dense growth of bushes and small trees. In fall, migrating swallows,
sometimes in the thousands, gather in this area before heading
south. In winter, a feeding station near the entrance, operated by
the Audubon people, draws chickadees, nuthatches, and nearly
every other bird that usually winters in the state. Over the course
of a year, about 150 species of birds frequent the little refuge.

The trails are blazed in yellow, blue, and red. Even with frequent
stops to observe the birds, you can easily walk all three paths in
1½ to 2 hours.

From the parking lot, only the yellow trail is visible. It starts
beside a large wooden sign, where trail maps are available, and
heads into a stand of pine and spruce, edging a small pond created
for wildlife. In spring and fall, you may find herons, bitterns,
sandpipers, and any of a half-dozen kinds of ducks.

Beyond the pines, you enter the old farm fields, now overgrown with bushes, many of which produce berries that attract numerous birds. Catbirds are abundant here, along with mockingbirds, thrashers, orioles, thrushes, and goldfinches. Quail and pheasants reside in the areas that are kept relatively open.

Quickly, you reach the blue-blazed trail, breaking off to the left. Follow it for your first look at the salt marshes. The first segment takes you through a dense thicket and over a narrow brook; then, when you reach the marsh, the trail forks. A side trail swings left, down to the edge of a small cove. During most of the year, you can expect to see shorebirds feeding in the shallows, particularly herons and big, white American and snowy egrets that are familiar figures throughout the area.

The main trail loops around the perimeter of a small peninsula, offering good views of the marshes and river at several high points. Dense shadbush and bayberry add color in early spring and attract even more birds (waxwings, titmice, cardinals) in summer.

When you return to the yellow trail, keep left for another circular walk on a higher peninsula. Here, you find more evidence that this birdland was once farmland. Several stone walls mark off forgotten fields, and an overgrown but still visible tractor lane twice cuts across the footpath.

The trail clings to the very edge of this point of lane, 8 to 10 feet above the water's surface. Although there are few tall trees, the undergrowth is extremely thick. Several openings do, however, provide good overlooks. When you notice the trail start curving back, take a side path down to the beach and the fiddler crabs. Walk the beach around the point for your best look at the tiny crabs, which are named for the one disproportionately large claw that resembles a base fiddle. Hundreds of tiny holes in the sand betray their presence and on warm, sunny days you are likely to see hundreds of them scurrying across the beach or hiding just inside their burrows. For many walkers, particularly those with small children, the fiddlers may be the highlight of Ruecker.

After you climb back up to the yellow trail, finish the loop until you reach the red-blazed path going off to the left. Turn and enter the deepest woods on the refuge. There still are few tall trees, but here you will find some oaks and hickories and a stand of alders. Alders frequently mean woodcocks, because these small trees thrive in the same moist ground where the long-billed birds probe for earthworms.

The red trail winds along low but unusual rock ledges. Small pebbles appear to be cemented together; local residents call it pudding stone. This sedimentary bedrock, estimated to be 250 million years old, is found few other places than the Narragansett Bay basin. A similar, though larger, mass formed Hanging Rock in the Norman Bird Sanctuary (see Walk 36).

These ledges do not extend far, however, and the trail soon swings right through dense woods (great for warblers and flycatchers), crosses the faint tractor road once more, then emerges at the parking lot.

36. Norman Bird Sanctuary

The largest range of bird species and a visit to Hanging Rock

Hiking distance: 3½ miles
Hiking time: 2 hours

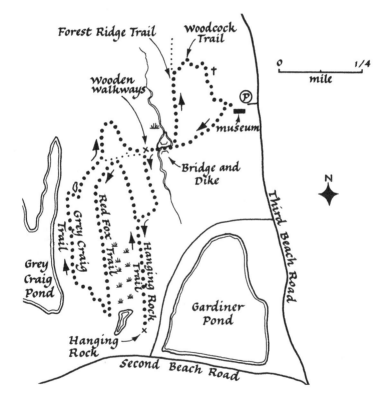

THE NORMAN BIRD SANCTUARY, EAST OF NEW-
port, is unique among Rhode Island walking areas for several
reasons. It is the only place that charges a fee for entering, but
some of its other qualities can make you feel the place is well worth
the cost.

Norman, a privately owned property, has a natural history
museum, there are usually live hawks or owls or other birds on the
premises recovering from injuries, and it is truly a sanctuary for
birds of all kinds. You may see more species of birds on these trails
than on any other in this book.

The trails wander back and forth over the refuge's 450 acres, and
on the 3½-mile walk described here you will travel three parallel
yet distinctive ridges. One leads to the famed Hanging Rock, from
which you can see over Gardiner Pond and the ocean beach. Another
offers views of Grey Craig Pond and its waterfowl. Other trails pass
through forests and around swamps, and one runs through a field
managed for woodcocks.

ACCESS

To reach the sanctuary from the west side of Narragansett Bay,
cross the Newport Bridge, take RI 138 and continue straight east,
via Miantonomi Avenue and Green End Avenue, until reaching
Third Beach Road. Go right (south) on Third Beach Road less than
1 mile. The refuge is on the right. From the east side of the bay,
drive RI 138 to Mitchells Lane, turn left and continue as Mitchells
becomes Third Beach Road.

Norman Bird Sanctuary is open all year, 9 a.m. to 5 p.m. Admis-
sion is charged and there are group rates available. The fee admits
you to the museum and the exhibits as well as to the trails. Pick
up a trail map before heading into the refuge.

TRAIL

The walk starts behind the museum buildings. Trails here are
not blazed in the usual manner — paint splotches on trees — but
there are numerous signs to keep you from getting lost. Follow the
main dirt road downhill, passing several signs for side trails, until
reaching a bridge. Extensive work has been done recently in this
area. This bridge is part of a concrete and wooden dam on an

earthen dike built to help regulate water in Red Maple Swamp, just to your right.

Beyond the dike, you will reach an intersection of several new wooden walkways over boggy areas. Look for the sign pointing the way to Hanging Rock, to the left. In a short distance, you reach a steep incline up the "pudding-stone" formations that make up nearly all of the first ridge. Pudding-stone is a rock mass composed of countless pebbles cemented together eons ago. It is common throughout the Narragansett Bay basin but relatively rare elsewhere.

The trail runs in two directions atop the ridge; Hanging Rock is to the left. For ¼ mile, you walk above the surrounding trees and hills. The walking is relatively easy, although the footing can be slippery when wet. The path ends abruptly at Hanging Rock, where you should pause and take in the views. To the left is Gardiner Pond, where geese and ducks often congregate in fall. Beyond is the Atlantic Ocean, which also can be seen straight ahead. To the right, far below, is a marshy area, then another rocky ridge.

Formerly, you could descend from Hanging Rock and cross the marshy region to the second ridge, but now it is too wet, so you have to return on the pudding-stone ridge, past the incline you climbed earlier, and downhill to a trail intersection.

Signs on a tree point to a blue trail, an orange trail, and one called Grey Craig Trail, marked in white. On your map, the blue trail is called Valley Trail and deadends in the marshy area you saw earlier. The orange trail is Red Fox Trail, which runs the crest of the second ridge. Take it; you'll come back on Grey Craig.

The second ridge is not quite as high as the first, and the cedars that grow through cracks in the rocks are somewhat taller. I remember walking this trail in November one year, and it seemed every robin in Rhode Island had gathered here, feeding on the cedar berries before heading south. Often cedar waxwings, white-throated sparrows and various warblers dally in this area, too.

When you reach the end of the ridge, you'll find a sign for Grey Craig Trail, curling down to the right. You walk briefly through a narrow, pretty valley, cross a wooden walkway, and them climb the third ridge.

Now you are starting back toward the center of the refuge. To the left is Grey Craig Pond, and the trail offers several good overlooks. In migration time, you are likely to see geese, several varieties of ducks, and often loons and other waterfowl here. Some ducks remain throughout the summer, when you also will see swans and shorebirds of several kinds. It is a good place to linger.

As you descend into the woods, the trail swings around a water hole and reaches another signpost beneath a magnificent beech tree. You have now walked about 2½ miles, and if you walked straight ahead you would be at the dike in a few moments. The Grey Craig Trail, however, goes left for a short swing through the woods before returning to the dike intersection.

After crossing the dike and bridge, you could return to your car, but I recommend swinging left on what is called the Forest Ridge Trail. It runs through open, pleasant woods with numerous stone walls and boulders. Turn off, to the right, on Woodcock Trail for a walk through an overgrown field now designed to lure woodcocks. The first time I walked through it, I nearly stepped on a woodcock that had been probing for worms right on the path. I haven't seen one there since, but I still keep looking.

The trail ends at a small family cemetery. Turn right, following a path along the sanctuary gardens, and in minutes you are back to the buildings and your car.

37. Cliff Walk

A walk along the Newport shoreline bluff for ocean views and marvelous mansions

Hiking distance: 6½ miles
Hiking time: 3 hours

SOONER OR LATER, EVERY RHODE ISLAND
walker has to try Cliff Walk. It is the state's most famous and most
walked trail, a 3¼-mile walkway that follows the Newport shoreline.
For the entire distance you have the sea on one side and the magnificent mansions of another time on the other.

In summer, this is a crowded walk, with numerous out-of-state
tourists using it to get a free look at the mansions, among the most
lavish homes ever built in America. The trail runs behind dozens
of these sixty- to seventy-room "summer cottages" built in the late
1800s when Newport was the playground of the Vanderbilts and
Astors, the Whartons and Belmonts, and other leaders of finance.
Many of these mansions, which face Bellevue Avenue, are now
open in the summer months as museum-like relics of a gilt-edged
era.

A crisp spring or autumn day might be best for this walk, because
not only is the trail crowded in summer, but also heat tends to
smudge the sea views. Also, there is virtually no shade for the entire
distance and most of the walkway is concrete or gravel, so a beating
sun can make the hiking too hot for you to get the most out of it.

ACCESS

To reach Cliff Walk's start, take RI 138 into Newport, turn south
on RI 138A or RI 214 and continue to Memorial Boulevard. Turn
right and you quickly reach the state-owned Easton Beach, where
you can park. There is room for several cars on the street. Parking
is limited to three hours, but you can walk the entire Cliff Walk
and return on foot in that time. The beach parking lot carries a fee
in summer but is free the rest of the year.

If you wish to make a one-way walk, you can place another car
on Ledge Road or Ocean Avenue near Cliff Walk's end. Take Memorial Boulevard to Bellevue, turn left, and drive past the mansions.
Ledge Road is a narrow street that runs to Land's End, where many
walkers conclude their trek. There is no parking allowed at the end
of the street, but there is room for a few cars farther up. Some
visitors walk to privately owned Bailey Beach on Ocean Avenue, a
short distance beyond Land's End, but there also is limited parking
at that site.

A simple solution might be to just walk back to Easton Beach.
If backtracking along Cliff Walk is undesirable, simply go out Ledge

Road and turn right on Bellevue Avenue. This way, you can see the front of some of the mansions as well as those on the opposite side of the street. Bellevue Avenue is shaded with immense beech trees and can be one of the most pleasant city strolls anywhere, eventually running by a shopping area and the famed Tennis Casino before reaching Memorial Boulevard. By street, the return is just over 3 miles, making a round-trip of about 6½ miles, rather easily done in 3 hours.

TRAIL

Starting at Easton Beach, walk uphill to Cliff Walk's start, just behind a restaurant called Cliff Walk Manor. Quickly, you rise high above the sea. The path is a sidewalk that twists and turns as it follows the shore. For the most part, fences or hedges, or both, line the right side. On the left is open ocean. To the far left, across a cove, you can see Middletown, Easton Point, and Sachuest Point.

In a matter of minutes, you reach Forty Steps, originally a natural rock formation leading down to the water, but now a concrete stairway and observation platform. Just beyond, the walkway was recently repaired with new retaining walls below the path. Erosion and constant battering by waves require frequent work on the path, and occasionally sections are closed to the public for brief periods. In such cases, detour routes on city streets are devised.

Beyond the first area, where you can see large buildings now part of Salve Regina College, you reach a permanently open iron gate. This is Cliff Walk's entrance to The Breakers, the Italian-style palace Cornelius Vanderbilt commissioned in 1895. A rose hedge, a wrought-iron fence, and a vast lawn separate the trail from the mansion, but several breaks in the hedge enable you to marvel at the awesome size of the seventy-room "cottage."

After passing a second iron gate and several more immense homes, the trail turns and climbs a few steps between cement and brick walls. Behind a high white wall on the right is Rosecliff, the famed mansion used in filming the movie "The Great Gatsby." Unfortunately, not much of the building can be seen from Cliff Walk.

Ahead loom some of the walk's better-known features, including a Chinese-style tea house almost directly above the trail. This was Mrs. Otto Belmont's tea room when she resided at Marble House. You will pass through a curving tunnel nearly beneath the pagoda,

For the length of Cliff Walk, you have the pounding sea on one side and opulent mansions on the other.

then swing left and pass through another short tunnel through a rocky ridge called Sheep Point.

You now leave the sidewalks behind. The path is gravel and dirt for some distance, then swings onto the jagged rocks of aptly named Rough Point. Below, on the left, are more large boulders in the water and they create fine shows of surf spray. Sections of the path have deteriorated, and care must be used in getting through.

At Rough Point, you cross a deep chasm on a wooden bridge, then cover another 100 yards of rough footing before the path goes up and follows the edge of an unfenced lawn. This area provides excellent views of several more huge homes built in European style.

When the trail breaks out onto a street, you are facing the last mansion on the route, Land's End, once the George Eustis Paine estate. The street is Ledge Road, and you turn right to reach your car or to walk back to Easton Beach. A path around the stone mansion would take you to Bailey Beach and Ocean Avenue.

38. Beavertail Park

An island walk through military and sailing history

Hiking distance: 3 miles
Hiking time: 2 hours

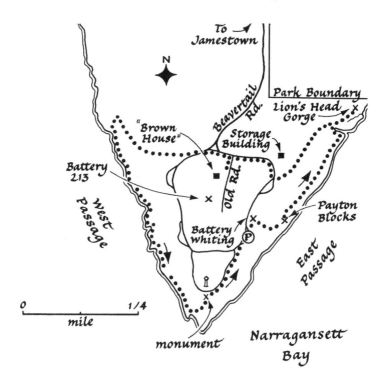

To Jamestown

N

Park Boundary

Lion's Head Gorge

Beavertail Rd.

"Brown House"

Storage Building

Battery 213

Old Rd.

West Passage

Payton Blocks

Battery Whiting

P

East Passage

monument

Narragansett Bay

0   1/4
mile

A WALK IN BEAVERTAIL STATE PARK IS ONE that can be fascinating at any time of year. And you don't have to wait for good weather. In fact, in many ways it is more alluring, more inspiring, in stormy weather.

Beavertail is located at the southern tip of Jamestown Island in Narragansett Bay. It is part of Rhode Island's new Bay Islands Park System and is still in the early stages of development. There are no marked hiking trails at the present, but a scenic and most interesting walk of about 3 miles can be made by following the rocky shoreline and cutting across the center of the park, while checking out numerous bits of military and sailing history.

ACCESS

Reaching the park is not difficult; only one road — Beavertail Road — runs due south out of the village of Jamestown. Follow it into the park, continue past the first few parking areas, swing around the lighthouse and park in the first lot just beyond. Here, overlooking the pounding surf, is the ideal place to begin and end your visit.

Once, this point was among the most notorious places in New England for sailors. Shipwrecks dot its history — more than 30 vessels have been destroyed or run aground here in the past 150 years — and when the waves are high and they crash onto the rocks below, it's easy to imagine how treacherous this place can be in a storm. In fact, you can still find a bit of cargo from a ship that went down in 1859.

In calmer weather, this is a place of beauty. Photographers and artists often can be found here, recording the white spray of the surf gleaming in the sunshine. Other visitors simply sit on the rocks and drink in the scenery.

TRAIL

You can walk either direction, but for this stroll, go left, east. From the parking lot, a narrow path runs into a thicket of bushes. In a few steps, you'll find the concrete facing of Battery Whiting, one of the bunkers established on Beavertail to protect Narragansett Bay during World War II. The bunker itself has now been sealed off but a few more steps to the left takes you to an observation station, which you can walk into. Gun placements just outside the station guarded the bay's East Passage.

155

After looking over these remnants of what was Fort Burnside, return to the parking lot, follow a path down to the shoreline rocks, and head east. In the distance, across the water, you can see Newport. The nimble can walk on the large but uneven rocks. There also is a faint path farther up the shore, where the grass meets the rocks. In this area, look for rectangular granite blocks among the rocks; these were destined for Alexandria, Virginia, aboard the H.F. Payton when it sank here well over a century ago after crashing into Shipwreck Rock. The building blocks rested beneath the waves until the hurricane of 1938 flung about a dozen of them onto the rocks. On close inspection you can see the flowery designs chiseled into the granite.

Throughout this section, there are good views, looking back, of the lighthouse. Many seabirds frequent this area — terns, cormorants and gulls in summer; scoters, eiders, and mergansers in winter.

Continue along the rocks, which soon turn from whitish to slate-gray, until you reach a deep chasm. This is Lion's Head Gorge. You can take a path up into the bushes and around the chasm a few more yards to see how the place got its name. At a point from which you can see the Newport Bridge, there is a jagged cleft in the rocks into which the tide flows, often resulting in a loud, crashing sound that reminded an early visitor of a lion's roar.

The path goes on beyond this point, but you would soon be leaving state property, so at the head of the chasm, take a narrow trail through the bushes back toward the lighthouse. This path runs to a parking lot (not the lot where you began). Turn right on the paved road, passing an outhouse, and follow the road as it circles inland. You will see a brown building with high radio antennae to the left and a metal, round-top storage building to the right.

An abandoned roadway runs toward the brown building, which looks like a house but was a special wartime structure built as an identification and communications center monitoring all incoming vessels. Great pains were taken to make the building resemble a summer cottage, but the walls are three feet thick, some of the "windows" were merely painted decorations, and the real windows were equipped with metal shields. The building is now a caretaker's home and off-limits to visitors.

Also near the abandoned road, between the brown building and the lighthouse, hidden in a tangle of tall bushes, is Battery 213, an underground complex used by the Navy during the war. During the summer months, a park naturalist conducts tours of the bunker, but visitors are advised not to attempt exploration on their own. The complex is in total darkness and holes in the floors make wandering around extremely dangerous.

Stay on the park road as it loops through the park interior. Pass the exit road and cross the road on which you entered. Beyond it, behind a stop sign, pick up a grassy lane that runs toward the ocean. It will jog to the right several times before reaching the shoreline. When you are at the water's edge, turn left on a narrow footpath.

For the rest of the way, you are following this path back toward the lighthouse. Much of the time, the path is at the very edge of cliffs above the jagged rocks and you have to make like a mountain goat in clinging to the trail. For those less agile, there are other paths farther back, in the bushes, but they offer less of a challenge and do not permit as many good views of the surf.

This side of Beavertail usually is more sheltered than the southern and eastern exposures, particularly in winter, and as such is a favorite place of birders, many of whom use the parking facilities just above. During stormy weather, flocks of brant, scaup, and other wintering ducks and geese rest on this side, and frequently rare birds seek refuge near this cliff. In summer, sandpipers feed on the rocks and there are always terns soaring by.

In the thick bushes above the water, numerous songbirds that usually migrate south — meadowlarks, robins, flickers, various sparrows — linger throughout the winter. You also are likely to see several species of hawks here.

Once you pass a tall wooden post, just as the lighthouse comes into view, the walking becomes easier, although you still have to swing inland around chasms a few times. You can climb down onto the rocks at several places, giving you a chance to look over the barnacles and other marine life found there, and perhaps feel the salt spray. Below the lighthouse you will cross one area covered with small, blue clam shells.

Climb back up to the road when you see a large foghorn installed beside a stone monument. The inscription notes that the spot is the site of Beavertail's first lighthouse, built in 1749, the third to be established on the Atlantic coast. Your car is a short distance to the right, but before leaving, take another look at the timeless ocean; it hasn't changed in all those years, yet it is never exactly the same on any two visits.

39. Block Island South

A visit to the famous Mohegan Bluffs on the southern end of historic Block Island

Hiking distance: 8½ miles
Hiking time: 3½-4 hours

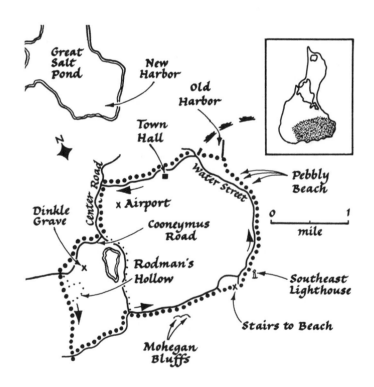

IF YOU ARE LOOKING FOR SOMETHING UNIQUE in your walk, take a trip to Block Island. Here you can walk for many miles and continue to see sights not available anywhere else in Rhode Island.

Block Island, 12 miles south of Rhode Island's mainland, once was a farming and fishing community. Later, it became something of a resort and vacation spot, earning the nickname "Bermuda of the North." The beaches and shops and restaurants still draw crowds in summer, but in autumn — the best time to visit the island — the place is still a wonderland of seascapes, cliffs, plant life, bird life, and history.

The walk described here — 8½ miles through the central and southeastern regions of the island, visiting the spectacular Mohegan Bluffs — is one of the more popular routes, although far more visitors use mopeds and bicycles than their feet. Except for the mile walk through an intriguing place called Rodman's Hollow, the distance is easily enough traveled on wheels, but I always have the feeling even mopeds and bikes are too fast; their riders miss too much.

ACCESS

As with our other Block Island hike (see Walk 40), this one begins and ends in the village of New Shoreham at Old Harbor, where the ferry boats from Point Judith and Providence drop off and pick up passengers.

With the walk taking 3½ to 4 hours, it may be best to take the Point Judith ferry, which takes only about an hour to reach the island. It leaves from a state pier in the village of Galilee. The Providence boat ride, which includes a stop in Newport, takes about three hours, which would not leave much time for walking if you plan to return the same day.

Schedules vary with the season and sometimes change within a season, so check departure times in advance. The ferry makes several round-trip runs each day during the summer, two daily in spring and fall, and just one a day in winter.

TRAIL

From the landing, turn right on the first street (Water Street),

159

going past the souvenir shops and the first of the large wooden hotels that were built when New Shoreham was in its heyday at the turn of the century. Turn left on Chapel Street and start uphill into a residential area. Shortly, Chapel Street merges with Old Town Road. You will pass the town hall and quickly reach the island's interior.

If you are used to forest walks, you'll be struck by the absence of tall trees on the island. Early settlers cut the trees in carving out their farms, and the ocean winds that buffet the island, frequently mercilessly in winter, prevent new vegetation from gaining much height.

Still, there is much greenery all around. Old fruit trees (apples, pears, peaches) line the first section of Old Town Road and many are now being engulfed by swarming grape vines. Bayberry bushes, blackberry vines, sumac, and wild roses form thickets — virtually impenetrable walls — along the roadway. Wildflowers are common and colorful.

When you reach Center Road, turn left and climb the steep hill. This road swings to the right around a little airport, where the gulls often outnumber planes on the runway. On the opposite side of the road, to your right, you have an open view across lowland moors to houses perched on hilltops along the western edge of the island.

At the next intersection, go right on Cooneymus Road, if you wish to walk through Rodman's Hollow. (If not prepared for the hollow's narrow path and its many briars, stay on Center Road as it becomes Lakeside Drive on its run to the southern shore. The two paths will eventually meet.)

The first house on Cooneymus Road, as a sign indicates, is called "Smilin' Through," for it was here that Arthur Penn composed the hit song of that name in the 1920s. Trustum Dodge, one of the original island settlers, also had a home at this site in the 1600s. The house is now a private museum.

After Cooneymus makes a sweeping curve to the left, you come upon a wooden turnstile set in a stone wall on the left. Beyond is a stone-walled rectangle with an iron gate. Inside is one tiny white headstone inscribed, "Dearly Beloved, Dinkle Mazzur." Nothing more.

Once this rectangle was a cemetery for early settlers, but years ago those buried here were moved to the island's central cemetery.

160

The Mazzur family bought the property and buried Dinkle here. He was their pet dog.

Shortly after the road turns right, you reach Rodman's Hollow, on your left. To the left of a sign that says "Walkers Welcome," a path drops down the steep slope into the deep hollow. Several trails run through this bushy ravine, but follow the most-used path that runs toward a pass between two ridges directly to the south. Surging bushes and clutching blackberry vines make the walking difficult in places, but it also can be a welcome relief from walking on roads, particularly when the day is hot and the traffic is heavy.

The hollow is supposedly one of the favorite haunts of the Block Island meadow vole, a mouse-like rodent found nowhere else on earth except this island. Hawks that feed on the vole and other small prey also are common in the hollow, along with numerous songbirds, especially during migration season.

When you reach a stone wall, the worn path goes uphill, to the left, then circles back toward Cooneymus Road. You should cross the low wall and continue on a narrower trail. It runs for half a mile and skirts several damp areas before emerging in a parking area near the shoreline bluffs. This is a delightful place to pause and rest, a hundred feet above the crashing surf.

A dirt road runs along the shore; take it, to the left. You soon will be walking between walls of bushes, with few good views of the ocean, until the lane curves left and reaches a paved road. This is the Mohegan Trail running above the island's most famous cliffs.

The bluffs were named for the Mohegan Indian war party driven over these cliffs by the island's Indians, the Manisseans, in 1590. The bluffs tower 160 feet above the beach and ocean, and you can reach these cliffs by two chief cutoffs. The first is a sandy lane running through the dunes from a point where the paved road makes a jog left. I like following the lane to the edge of the cliff, which offers good views of the shoreline to the right and a lighthouse to the left. Then, I follow a faint path along the rim to a ravine across from a wooden stairway that descends to the beach. This path also goes down the ravine — be careful, it can be slippery — offering a look at the cliffs from below.

When ready to resume the walk, climb the long, 160-step stairs, detour to the right a few yards to an observation platform, then return to the paved road. Ahead looms Southeast Lighthouse, which carries a beam ships can see for 30 miles. Near the light is a stone that lists the names of 16 ships that were wrecked along this shore, ending with the chilling suffix "etc."

You are now on Southeast Light Road, heading back toward the village. The road name is soon changed to Spring Street. Where the road runs next to the water, you may want to leave the pavement, cross the guardrail, and follow a path down to the beach. This is aptly-named Pebbly Beach, and a short walk on it takes you to an inn, an excellent place to refresh yourself while awaiting your ferry.

40. Block Island North

A varied walk along the more peaceful side of historic Block Island — a special place for rare bird sightings

Hiking distance: 9½ miles
Hiking time: 4-4½ hours

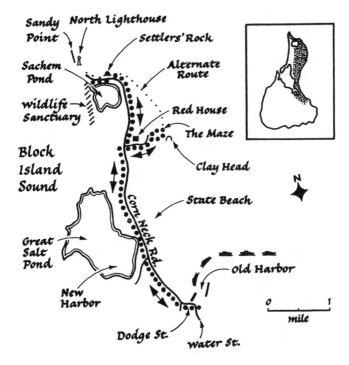

Sandy Point
North Lighthouse
Settlers' Rock
Sachem Pond
Alternate Route
Wildlife Sanctuary
Red House
The Maze
Block Island Sound
Clay Head
Corn Neck Rd.
State Beach
Great Salt Pond
Old Harbor
New Harbor
Dodge St.
Water St.
N
0   1
mile

THE NORTHERN END OF BLOCK ISLAND OFFERS

the walker a wide variety of sights: a flotilla of boats and a lovely, quiet pond; a sand dune wildlife sanctuary and a dense jungle-like thicket; a low-lying spit of land and high cliffs.

This walk also offers less crowded areas than most of the island, which attracts increasingly large numbers of visitors and vacationers in summer. It is a long walk, well over 9 miles if you spend much time rambling in the thicket called The Maze, but it is an easy stroll, nearly all of it on one paved road except for The Maze.

As with the Block Island South hike (Walk 39), this route begins and ends at the ferry landing at Old Harbor in New Shoreham. The walk, however, is not a loop but a simple return on the same road, since there is only one road that runs to the northern tip, the place where white settlers first arrived on the island.

ACCESS

This walk takes approximately 4 hours, so it may be best to take the Point Judith ferry, which actually leaves from a state pier in the village of Galilee. The 12-mile trip takes only about an hour each way, as opposed to the three-hour ride on the ferry from Providence. Six hours on the ferry would not leave much time for walking if you intend to spend only one day.

Schedules vary with the season and sometimes change within a season, so check departure times in advance. The ferry makes several round-trip runs each day during the summer, two daily in spring and fall and just one a day in winter.

TRAIL

From the landing at Old Harbor, go right on Water Street, past the souvenir shops and the large wooden hotels that were built when New Shoreham was the "Bermuda of the North" at the turn of the century. Turn left on Dodge Street, then, at the island post office, turn right on Corn Neck Road and you are all set. Corn Neck Road runs all the way to Settlers' Rock at the island's northern tip.

You could also walk on the beach in this section — it's smooth sand for well over 1 mile — but this is a long walk and the sand may make you too weary too soon. The road is easier, even though

164

you often have to contend with cars, mopeds, and bicycles headed for New Harbor or the state beach.

Shortly after you begin, you will see one of the many historical monuments scattered around the island, this one noting the murder of a Boston trader, John Oldham, by Indians in 1636. Historical insights make most walks more interesting and Block Island has history all around.

Soon, you are able to see the masts of sailboats moored in Great Salt Pond to your left, then you will pass the state beach pavilion on your right. As you proceed, the views of the large pond improve, and in summer, when New Harbor is filled with boats (many of them large and luxurious) the panoramic vista is a delight for sailing enthusiasts.

Once past the pond, the road runs between old fields that have returned to bushes. There are some old farmhouses here and many new cottages, but the walk is usually uneventful for 1 mile or so. Still, it can be surprising. On one walk in this area, I found a yellow-headed blackbird, a species rare in New England and one I had never seen on mainland Rhode Island.

Rare birds seem drawn to Block Island, and each October birders from around the nation flock here. Many migratory birds use the island as a resting place and seabirds that seldom visit the mainland seek refuge here during storms. The increase in birds as well as the decrease in crowds and traffic make autumn the ideal time to walk the island.

About 3 miles from your start is a side road that runs to The Maze, a privately owned thicket in which the owners have cut 11 miles of narrow, winding trails. If you so desire, you can spend an entire day wandering these trails, but if you also want to reach Settlers' Rock, it might be advisable simply to follow the trail that runs to Clay Head, the high cliff on the island's eastern shore, and then return to the paved road. If you wish, you also can follow a path that runs north (left) from Clay Head along the shoreline all the way to Settlers' Rock. It's a pretty stretch but adds considerable distance and time to your walk.

Finding The Maze is not easy; there are no signs along Corn Neck Road. Look for a red house and electrical pole No. 129 on the right, beside a dirt road. Follow the dirt road a few hundred yards, then watch for small signs that indicate the route to the

Lapham family property. The Laphams created The Maze and allow walkers to use it. On the path to Clay Head, you are likely to see dozens of songbirds and perhaps a deer or two.

Back on Corn Neck Road, the pavement rises, offering good views to the left of Block Island Sound. From the highest hilltop, on a clear day, you also may be able to see (on your left) Gardiner's Island and Fisher's Island, part of New York State, as well as some of the Connecticut shoreline. Ahead is mainland Rhode Island and off to the right is the Massachusetts shore — four states from one spot.

There are a few taller trees lining the road as you head downhill. In minutes, you arrive at Sachem Pond, a picturesque pond that, along with the rugged dunes on the opposite shore, makes up a wildlife sanctuary. The dunes are the nesting site of numerous gulls, terns, and other birds.

Corn Neck Road ends at Settlers' Rock, a monument on the northern end of Sachem Pond. The rock commemorates the arrival, in 1661, of the 16 Boston men who became the first permanent white inhabitants of the island. Near the rock, which is 4 miles from your start not counting your detour through The Maze, are picnic tables and a small beach on the pond side, making it an excellent place to rest.

The ambitious can continue, however, as a sandy lane runs farther out on the point, to North Lighthouse, a non-operating landmark planned for restoration. Beyond the light is Sandy Point, a narrow, sometimes submerged sand bar that has been the scene of a great many shipwrecks over the centuries.

Sooner or later, though, you will have to leave this alluring area and head back toward the ferry. Keep in mind, from Settlers' Rock it's a 4-mile walk. Make sure you give yourself enough time. The one thing you don't want to do on Block Island is hurry.

Guidebooks from The Countryman Press and Backcountry Publications

Written for people of all ages and experience, these popular and carefully prepared books feature detailed trail and tour directions, notes on points of interest and natural phenomena, maps and photographs.

Walks and Rambles Series
Walks and Rambles on the Delmarva Peninsula, $9.95
Walks and Rambles in Dutchess and Putnam Counties (NY), $9.95
Walks and Rambles in Rhode Island, $8.95
Walks and Rambles in the Upper Connecticut River Valley, $9.95
Walks and Rambles in Westchester (NY) and Fairfield (CT) Counties, $7.95

Biking Series
25 Mountain Bike Tours in Vermont, $9.95
25 Bicycle Tours on Delmarva, $8.95
25 Bicycle Tours in Eastern Pennsylvania, $8.95
20 Bicycle Tours in the Finger Lakes, $8.95
20 Bicycle Tours in the 5 Boroughs (NYC), $8.95
25 Bicycle Tours in the Hudson Valley, $9.95
25 Bicycle Tours in Maine, $9.95
25 Bicycle Tours in New Hampshire, $7.95
25 Bicycle Tours in New Jersey, $8.95
20 Bicycle Tours in and around New York City, $7.95
25 Bicycle Tours in Ohio's Western Reserve, $9.95
25 Bicycle Tours in Vermont, $8.95

Canoeing Series
Canoe Camping Vermont and New Hampshire Rivers, $7.95
Canoeing Central New York, $10.95
Canoeing Massachusetts, Rhode Island and Connecticut, $7.95

Hiking Series
50 Hikes in the Adirondacks, $11.95
50 Hikes in Central New York, $9.95
50 Hikes in Central Pennsylvania, $9.95
50 Hikes in Eastern Pennsylvania, $10.95
50 Hikes in the Hudson Valley, $9.95
50 Hikes in Massachusetts, $11.95
50 More Hikes in New Hampshire, $9.95
50 Hikes in New Jersey, $10.95
50 Hikes in Northern Maine, $10.95
50 Hikes in Ohio, $12.95
50 Hikes in Southern Maine, $10.95
50 Hikes in Vermont, $11.95
50 Hikes in West Virginia, $9.95
50 Hikes in Western New York, $11.95
50 Hikes in Western Pennsylvania, $11.95
50 Hikes in the White Mountains, $12.95

Adirondack Series
Discover the Adirondack High Peaks, $14.95
Discover the Central Adirondacks, $8.95
Discover the Eastern Adirondacks, $9.95
Discover the Northeastern Adirondacks, $9.95
Discover the Northern Adirondacks, $10.95
Discover the Northwestern Adirondacks, $12.95
Discover the South Central Adirondacks, $10.95
Discover the Southeastern Adirondacks, $8.95
Discover the Southern Adirondacks, $10.95
Discover the Southwestern Adirondacks, $9.95
Discover the West Central Adirondacks, $13.95

Ski-Touring Series
25 Ski Tours in Central New York, $7.95
25 Ski Tours in New Hampshire, $8.95

Other Guides
Maine: An Explorer's Guide, $14.95
New England's Special Places, $12.95
New Jersey's Special Places, $12.95
New York State's Special Places, $12.95
Pennsylvania Trout Streams and their Hatches, $14.95
State Parks and Campgrounds in Northern New York, $9.95
Vermont: An Explorer's Guide, $14.95
Waterfalls of the White Mountains, $14.95

The above titles are available at bookstores and at certain sporting goods stores or may be ordered directly from the publisher. For complete descriptions of these and other guides, write: The Countryman Press, P.O. Box 175, Woodstock, VT 05091.